International Commodity Markets

and the

Role of Cartels

International Commodity Markets

and the

Role of Cartels

MARK S. LeCLAIR

M.E. Sharpe

Armonk, New York
London, England

Library of Congress Cataloging-in-Publication Data

LeClair, Mark S.
    International commodity markets and the role of cartels / Mark S. LeClair.
      p. cm.
    Includes bibliographical references and index.
    ISBN 0-7656-0516-3 (hc. : alk. paper)
    1. Cartels. 2. Raw materials 3. International economic relations. I. Title.

HD2757.5 .L43 2000
338.8′7—dc21   00-025510

Printed in the United States of America

In memory of
Thomas J. LeClair
and
George W. Doornbosch

Contents

List of Tables and Figures

TABLES

Figures

Preface

In April 1999, petroleum prices slid to near-historic lows, and OPEC was spurred to cut production and firm prices. The doubling of oil prices between April and November of that year—from $12.50 to $25 per barrel—reminded the industrialized nations of the cartel's renewed capacity to control the market. As the price of petroleum rose, the U.S. government was called on to reverse the trend by releasing part of its stockpile onto the open market. Prior to OPEC's recent maneuvers, it had seemed that the collusive agreement, a market device for manipulating commodity prices so common in the 1970s and early 1980s, was merely an intriguing episode of trade relations.

The history of cartels actually dates back to the early twentieth century, when multinational corporations collaborated on the production of raw materials to secure higher prices. One looks to the events of 1901, for example, when the major producers of aluminum (Alcoa of the United States, AIAG of Switzerland, and Froges of France) agreed not to export to each other's markets, thereby effectively creating domestic monopolies. In 1920, British firms in the ranks of the Rubber Growers Association agreed to cut production by 25 percent in order to bring about higher prices. Similarly, in 1931, seven sugar-exporting nations signed a five-year plan of production and export quotas designed to improve market conditions. In that same year, the five major producers of tin agreed to a set of production carryovers and supply restrictions for the purpose of firming prices. The success of these agreements varied widely, with some of the cartels (notably those for tin) surviving for many decades.

The cartelization process gained momentum after World War II, with sugar and tin producers signing collusive agreements in the 1950s and the other primary commodity exporters following suit. But the reception of these market interventions soon became drawn along the lines of the relative level of industrialization in the countries involved. Recognizing the potential harm that such trade pacts could cause in their industrial sectors, the developed world—first the United States and then Europe and Canada—soon legislated antitrust laws to prevent collusion by multinational companies. Long recognized as major impediments to competition, cartels now became a key target of law enforcement officials in the industrialized nations. Despite these regulations, secret agreements on the division of market shares were periodically uncovered. In the United States, the most notorious violation of domestic trade law occurred in the electrical transformer industry in the 1950s. Large fines and jail time for the executives involved sent a stern message to corporations of the price to be paid for collusion.

It was not until the 1960s that the concept of cartels assumed center stage in international business circles, particularly under the aegis of The United Nations Conference on Trade and Development (UNCTAD). Concerned that the production and export of commodities had become centralized in the developing world and that the price of these goods relative to manufactured products had declined significantly, this commission, at least initially, elicited the support of both developed and developing countries in changing the terms of trade. As will be discussed in chapter 1, UNCTAD announced in its protocol of 1976 the intention of expanding cartelization beyond the primary commodities to products such as bananas, iron ore, meat, and vegetable oils. Western Europe, Japan, and the United States, apprehensive about the extension of collusive agreements to so many products and fearful of the elevation of prices that were already being realized, soon recoiled from UNCTAD's initiatives. Ultimately, it was without the support of the industrialized world that the Group of 77 developing nations (G-77) pursued cartelization through the United Nations and its agencies. The formation of collusive agreements under the UNCTAD plan then became part of a broader effort to establish a so-called "New Economic Order" in international trade.

Although UNCTAD's market strategies created a sense of excitement about the potential benefits of cartels, their implementation was fraught with problems from the start. As detailed in chapter 1, the difficulties that developed in the newly forged agreements for bauxite, cocoa, coffee, petroleum, rubber, sugar, and tin can be attributed to the fact that most of these commodities fail to conform to one or more of the characteristics necessary for successful cartelization. By the mid-1980s, the collusive arrangements for these goods had dissolved and the interna-

tional trade of agricultural products, minerals, and petroleum had returned to free markets. The recent success of OPEC might suggest that a
renewal of the cartel process is under way in the developing world, but
the underlying incompatibility of these exports to collusive measures
remains. In addition, the price increases brought about by market manipulations encourage cartel members to violate their commitments to
one another and seek greater market shares.

Another factor working against the cohesiveness of cartels is the trend
in the past fifteen years or so toward diversification of the export structure of many developing nations. Colombia, Indonesia, and Malaysia,
for example, which used to rely heavily on single-commodity exporting
for their trade revenues, now produce a broad range of products. The
dislocations suffered by nations dependent on a sole product for their
foreign earnings are discussed in chapter 2, where it is demonstrated
that when the link between commodity prices and growth is broken, as
it was in the 1990s, the attractiveness of cartels wanes.

Chapter 3 provides an examination of the most important commodity
cartels of the last three decades. The means by which each cartel attempted to regulate production and prices, as well the market influences
that eventually led to their collapse, will be studied.

The relationship between cartels and commodity futures markets is
also examined in chapter 3. Essentially, futures markets provide a means
of stabilizing commodity prices without resorting to the formation of a
cartel. In fact, it can be demonstrated that when functioning cartels are
in place and prices are less volatile, trading volume on the various futures exchanges falls. The forward markets, however, are not effective
substitutes for cartels, for while they reduce price variability and provide certainty, they do not alter the deteriorating terms of trade faced by
developing nations.

The widespread economic dislocations caused by the commodity
price inflation of the 1970s form the focus of chapter 4. Most of the
market instability of the period can be traced to the so-called oil shocks,
which touched nearly every sector of the industrialized nations, but
other commodities played their role in the acceleration of inflation at
the wholesale level. Also to be considered is the effect that general
commodity inflation had on consumers. It will be argued that cooperation between importers and exporters of petroleum and other raw
materials benefits everyone.

The near-complete failure of the cartel movement, particularly the trend toward lower relative prices for commodities, is driving the search for alternative means of stabilizing export earnings. Chapter 5 outlines some of the programs—most in the industrialized world—that have sought to improve the terms of trade of developing nations. Under the most ambitious of these, Stabilization of Exchange (STABEX), which was initiated by the European Union in 1975, subsidies are provided to exporting nations when the world price of commodities falls short of a predetermined target price.

Even more aggressive means of addressing the trade dilemmas of the developing world will be presented in chapter five. Among these is the growing trend toward regional cooperation through trade integration. These free trade areas, particularly those in Latin America, embrace regional industrial planning and development, as well as export promotion. For nations that produce and export raw materials, these common markets provide a solution to the problem of the destructive competition that has long plagued commodity markets.

Another approach to the trade difficulties faced by developing nations involves the vertical integration of production, that is, the processing of commodities into finished or semifinished goods for trade. This attenuated hold on indigenous resources would enable exporters to capture a greater share of the value-added of their products, but this plan does not work for all commodities. Cocoa, coffee, and sugar producers, for example, cannot vertically integrate because their products are destined for consumption with only minimal processing. After the increased costs of production, transportation, and marketing, the exporters of cocoa beans, for instance, would realize very little return in expanding their operations to include chocolate exporting. Thus, although some benefits may accrue from processing raw materials prior to export, this is an approach not available to many developing nations.

Chapter 5 will also explore the few cartels that have managed to successfully manipulate prices over the long term. DeBeers Corporation, in particular, has controlled the diamond market for over a century by forcing buyers and sellers to trade through a central selling point or face retribution. As a result of this absolute centralization of trade, diamond prices are unhindered by the market pressures of competition, but such clearinghouses run counter to the principles of free trade.

Since the mid-1980s, the industrialized world has benefited from a period of gradually declining prices for most key commodities. But the halcyon days of consumerism may be numbered, as the combined forces of increasing global industrialization and expanding world population exert growing pressure on supplies of raw materials. A means of achieving long-term stability of commodity prices would benefit both producing and consuming nations and help prevent the type of economic dislocations that the world suffered in the 1970s.

Acknowledgments

I am grateful for the intellectual and financial support that I received at all stages of preparing this manuscript. The financial assistance extended to me by the Research Committee at Fairfield University enabled me to devote the summer of 1999 to collecting the data for the book. I would like to thank my colleagues in the Department of Economics at Fairfield University for their ongoing encouragement of my research endeavors. As in the past, our department secretary, Sally Williams, provided invaluable help in the production of this work. I thank the staff of Nyselius Library at Fairfield University for obtaining needed reference materials.

I am indebted to my family for their understanding and support during the researching and writing of this manuscript. A special word of thanks goes to my wife, Kathy Doornbosch, who served as my copy editor and sounding board throughout the project.

Abbreviations Used in Text

ACP	African, Caribbean, and Pacific Nations under STABEX
ASEAN	Association of Southeast Asian Nations
ATO	Alternative Trade Organization
CARICOM	Caribbean Community
CRB	Commodity Research Bureau
CSCE	New York Coffee, Sugar, and Cocoa Exchange
ECU	European Currency Unit
EPCA	Energy Policy and Conservation Act
IPC	Integrated Program for Commodities
IBA	International Bauxite Association
ICA	International Coffee Agreement
ICO	International Coffee Organization
ICCA	International Cocoa Agreement
IMF	International Monetary Fund
IRA	International Rubber Agreement
ISA	International Sugar Agreement
ITA	International Tin Agreement
KRE	Japan's KOBE Rubber Exchange
LAIA	Latin American Integration Association
OPEC	Organization of Petroleum Exporting Countries
SPR	Strategic Petroleum Reserve
STABEX	Stabilization of Exchange
TOCOM	Tokyo Commodity Exchange
UNCTAD	United Nations Conference on Trade and Development

International
Commodity
Markets
and the
Role of Cartels

1

International Commodity Markets and the Rise of Cartels

History has shown that cartelization can occur within any market where production is confined to a limited number of suppliers. Prior to the stricter enforcement of antitrust legislation in the industrialized world, corporations from the United States, Europe, and Canada regarded cartels as a reasonable means of increasing profitability in competitive international markets. Even after collusion became explicitly illegal, firms still engaged in the practice if the risks of getting caught were thought to be sufficiently low. Such was the case with the electrical transformer industry, which was briefly cartelized in the 1950s. Similarly, three executives of the Archer Daniels Midland Company (including the executive vice president) engaged in ongoing price-fixing of their food products during the 1980s, a practice that eventually caught up with them when they were prosecuted by the U.S. Department of Justice in 1998.

In contrast to these examples, however, the majority of cartels involve producers of commodity products, notably raw materials and high-return agricultural goods. The structure of international trade within these markets results in a strong interest in collusive agreements as a means of controlling prices. Production of many key commodities—including bauxite, cocoa, coffee, petroleum, rubber, and tin—is centered in the developing world, where legal barriers to the formation of cartels are either weak or nonexistent. Moreover, the economies of these producing nations are often dependent on foreign sales of only one or two commodities, a factor that creates an additional incentive to forge collusive arrangements as a means of maintaining prices.

The current pattern of commodity trade is largely the result of the combined effects of colonialism and the center-periphery relationship between developed and developing nations. As the industrial revolution progressed, new sources of raw materials were continually sought. Many of the key reserves of mineral and agricultural resources were located in the nonindustrialized nations of Africa, South America, and the Pacific Rim, and their economies became dependent on the extraction and sale of these raw materials. The efforts of international institutions (notably the World Bank) to eliminate the dependency of struggling nations on single-export trade—mainly through financial incentives such as long-term lending—have been unsuccessful.

THE PATTERNS OF WORLD COMMODITY PRODUCTION

The following analysis considers the world production patterns for seven key commodities that have been subject to cartelization. Markets in which cartels have been formed share two characteristics: Production is centered in the developing world and overproduction remains a perennial problem. Paradoxically, these market elements both encourage the formation of cartels and ultimately lead to their demise.

The International Coffee Market

Coffee production is centered in the developing nations of Africa and Latin America. World coffee output rose over 61 percent between 1974 and 1997, from 62.5 million to 100.9 million 60-kilogram bags. Brazil and Colombia command over one-third of this total; thus adverse crop conditions experienced there have an immediate impact on the world market (Table 1.1). With the exception of Ethiopia, African producers have declined in importance while Indonesian growers have captured a larger market share.

As in other commodity markets, coffee production has suffered the effects of oversupply. The ending stocks of the exporting nations reached 50.2 million bags in 1989, a figure that represented a high of 53.2 percent of total production (as compiled by the Commodity Research Bureau [CRB] in its *Commodity Yearbook*). In 1989, the total stockpile had risen to 50.2 million bags. Ending stocks declined to 28.5 percent in 1997, a figure that represented a total stockpile of 28.8 million bags, the lowest level since 1979, when stocks stood at just 26.0 million bags. As the reserves of coffee continue to decline, it would appear that producers are making progress toward more stable prices and a more quiescent market.

Table 1.1

Coffee Production, 1974 and 1997 (in thousands of 60-kg. bags and as a percentage of world output)

Key Producer	1974	(%)	1997	(%)
Brazil	14,500	23.2	27,000	26.8
Colombia	7,800	12.5	12,500	12.4
Costa Rica	1,570	2.5	2,500	2.5
Ethiopia	1,700	2.7	3,900	3.9
Guatemala	2,200	3.5	3,617	3.6
Indonesia	2,750	4.4	7,500	7.4
Ivory Coast	3,285	5.3	4,000	4.0
Mexico	3,300	5.3	5,400	5.4
Uganda	3,100	5.0	3,700	3.7

Source: CRB, *Commodity Yearbook.*
Note: Percentages do not total 100 percent because only key producers are included.

The International Rubber Market

The production and export of natural rubber represents the most complex of the international commodity markets, for unlike other products such as coffee and sugar, there is a near-perfect substitute: petroleum-derived synthetic rubber. Although there are certain uses for which natural rubber is preferred to synthetics, a significant degree of cross-substitution is nonetheless possible. In fact, synthetics make up over 60 percent of world rubber production, and thus their manufacture and pricing greatly affect the natural-rubber market.

Before the 1990s, the natural rubber market had been dominated by three Southeast Asian producers—Indonesia, Malaysia, and Thailand. In 1974, these nations produced nearly three-fourths of total world output of natural rubber. By 1994, however, a significant shift had taken place in the relative importance of these exporters (Table 1.2). Malaysia, which had been responsible for over 40 percent of world production in 1974, saw its share of world output cut to less than 20 percent. Conversely, during the same period, Thailand nearly tripled its share of total output, from 10.1 percent in 1974 to 30.1 percent. Since 1994, China and India have emerged as major new producers.

As for the synthetic rubber market, it has long been dominated by the United States, which maintained over one-fourth of world production between 1974 and 1994. Other major producers, ranked by their per-

Table 1.2

Rubber Production, 1974 and 1994 (in thousands of metric tons and as a percentage of world output)

Key Producer	1974	(%)	1994	(%)
Natural				
China	[1]	[1]	341.0	6.0
India	128.4	3.4	464.0	8.1
Indonesia	855.0	22.7	1,360.8	23.8
Malaysia	1,525.0	40.5	1,100.6	19.2
Sri Lanka	132.0	3.5	105.3	1.8
Thailand	379.5	10.1	1,722.4	30.1
Synthetic				
Canada	208.0	2.2	232.0	2.6
Germany	371.8	4.0	642.0	7.3
Japan[1]	[1]	[1]	1,349.0	15.3
United States	2,396.0	25.7	2,390.0	27.1
United Kingdom	335.8	3.6	290.7	3.3

Source: CRB, *Commodity Yearbook.*
[1]Not a significant producer in that year.

centage of world output, include Japan (15.3 percent), Germany (7.3 percent), the United Kingdom (3.3 percent), and Canada (2.6 percent).

The synthetic rubber market is tangential to this study not only because it is a substitute good, but also because, unlike raw materials, synthetics are typically produced and then utilized in the same market. Moreover, unlike many other commodities where production is subject to the vagaries of nature, the manufacture of synthetic rubber responds directly to market demands. Consequently, the major producers of artificial rubber are free from the instabilities that face the exporters of natural rubber.

The natural-rubber market, on the other hand, was subject to significant overproduction during the 1970s and early 1980s. From 1971 to the present, world buffer stocks (about 60 percent of which are held in consuming countries) have exceeded 1 million metric tons; in 1985 alone, 1.4 million metric tons of natural rubber were stockpiled. Thereafter, a steep decline in reserves began, with holdings falling by over 10 percent between 1985 and 1986. According to the most recent data (compiled in 1994), overproduction has ceased to be a significant problem, with output exceeding demand by only 80,000 metric tons (1.4 percent of total demand). Thus the world rubber market has experienced production and

Table 1.3

Tin Production, 1974 and 1995 (in thousands of metric tons and as a percentage of world output)

Key Producer	1974	(%)	1995	(%)
Australia	10.5	4.5	8.2	4.4
Bolivia	29.5	12.7	14.4	7.7
Brazil	4.4	1.9	16.8	9.0
Former USSR	29.5	12.7	—	—
Russia	—	—	9.0	5.3
China	20.0	8.6	52.0	27.8
Indonesia	25.0	10.7	38.4	20.5
Malaysia	68.1	29.2	6.4	3.4
Peru	1	1	22.3	11.9
Thailand	20.3	8.7	3.0	1.6

Source: U.S. Bureau of Mines.
[1] Not a significant producer in that year.

demand patterns very similar to those observed in the international coffee market, for in both cases the persistent excess production of the period from 1970 to 1985 has subsided, and more stable market conditions have emerged.

The International Tin Market

The production and export of tin is subject to far greater volatility than the other commodity markets. In the space of twenty-five years, the total output of tin declined by 24 percent, from 246,000 metric tons in 1980 to just 187,000 metric tons by 1995. In addition, a significant reorientation of production took place between 1974 and 1995, when many of the traditional exporters were eclipsed by formerly minor producers (Table 1.3). Thus in 1974, Malaysia, the former USSR, and Bolivia were the top producers of tin, with 29.2 percent, 12.7 percent, and 12.7 percent of the market, respectively; by 1995, however, China, Indonesia, and Peru had seized the top standings, with market shares of 27.8 percent, 20.5 percent, and 11.9 percent, respectively. Indeed, during this period, Malaysia's production had plummeted to a scant 3.4 percent of world output.

The instability of the tin market is a consequence of the commodity's significant price variability, coupled with the exhaustion of traditional reserves. World production peaked in 1980, when tin also saw its highest price of $16,743 per metric ton. By 1986, however, prices had fallen a precipitous 63 percent, to $6,149 per metric ton, and they deteriorated further, hitting bottom in 1993, when tin was selling for only $5,157 per metric ton. The collapse in tin prices resulted in significant economic pressures on producing nations, many of which voluntarily curtailed production to firm up prices. In the absence of a dramatic price recovery, it seems unlikely that these nations will elevate production to former levels.

The International Bauxite Market

The bauxite market is unique in both its production and its pricing. Unlike most commodities, the reserves of bauxite—the major commercial source of aluminum, consisting of hydrated alumina combined with iron oxides and other impurities—do not occur solely in the developing world but can also be found in Australia, France, Hungary, Greece, Russia, the United States, and Yugoslavia. Yet with the exception of Australia, the vast majority of world production takes place in developing nations— notably Brazil, Guinea, Guyana, India, Jamaica, and Suriname.

For the purposes of illustration, bauxite production will be considered for only two years, 1974 and 1995 (Table 1.4). One can see from the figures that Australia's market share has grown exponentially, from 25.1 percent to 39 percent. In 1974, Jamaica, Guinea, and Suriname were the most important suppliers among the developing nations. While the former two continue to retain a significant share of the world market, Suriname's output has fallen to just over 3 percent of global production. During the same timeframe, Brazil, China, and India, all minor producers in 1974, have become important market players.

Although the bauxite market was subject to a degree of overproduction in the early 1980s, the problem was not as severe as that affecting other commodities. This situation is due, in part, to the unusual pricing mechanism for the bauxite mined in the developing world, wherein the multinational firms that extract the mineral are obliged to pay the host country a levy on each ton of bauxite produced.

Another factor that could potentially affect aluminum production has to do with the status of bauxite as a strategic mineral. It is owing to its value as a building material in aeronautics that the United States has maintained a significant stockpile of bauxite for use in the event of war. These stocks have remained fairly stable for the last thirty years, with

Table 1.4

World Bauxite Production, 1974 and 1995 (in thousands of metric tons and as a percentage of world output)

Key Producer	1974	(%)	1995	(%)
Australia	20,073	25.1	42,655	39.0
Brazil	[1]	[1]	8,761	8.0
China	[1]	[1]	5,000	4.6
Guinea	7,630	9.5	14,400	13.2
India	[1]	[1]	4,800	4.4
Jamaica	15,388	19.1	10,857	10.0
Suriname	6,732	8.4	3,300	3.0

Source: U.S. Geological Service.
[1] Not a significant producer in that year.

the number of metric tons stored ranging from 14,661 in the early 1980s to 18,472 in the mid-1980s (CRB *Commodity Yearbook*). From time to time, the U.S. government has released bauxite from its stocks, thereby exerting downward pressure on the international price of aluminum. As this stockpile represents over a year of total U.S. demand, its potential impact on world bauxite prices is great.

The International Sugar Market

The production of sugar is widely dispersed among both developing and developed nations. In 1997, the two largest producers, Brazil and India, were responsible for over 25 percent of world output. Several industrialized nations—notably France, Germany, and the United States—were also important producers. Although the relative importance of the major producers has changed somewhat in the period between 1974 and 1997, the redistribution of output has been less significant than in other commodity markets (Table 1.5). During this period, Brazil, China, India, and especially Thailand increased their share of world production. Cuba and the nations of the former Soviet Union, on the other hand, are the only producers to have experienced meaningful declines. As for the United States, its production increased by nearly 2.3 million metric tons, yet its share of total output remained stable. At least in part, increased U.S. production can be attributed to continued government subsidies to the sugar industry.

The sugar market has been in a state of perpetual excess supply. Indeed, since 1974, total world supply has increased by 55 percent, from 80.5 mil-

Table 1.5

Sugar Production, 1974 and 1997 (in thousands of metric tons and as a percentage of world output)

Key Producer	1974	(%)	1997	(%)
Brazil	6,959	8.6	14,500	11.6
China	2,065	2.6	7,000	5.6
Cuba	5,800	7.2	4,600	3.7
France	3,255	4.0	4,400	3.5
India	4,949	6.1	17,000	13.6
Germany (West)	2,500	3.1	—	—
Germany	—	—	4,550	3.6
Mexico	2,805	3.5	4,600	3.7
Thailand	1	1	6,500	5.2
Former USSR	9,568	11.9	—	—
United States	4,171	5.2	6,468	5.2

Source: Foreign Agricultural Service, USDA.
[1]Not a significant producer in that year.

lion metric tons to 125.0 million metric tons. Even the small reduction in Cuba's output—the only decline reported among the major producers—was offset by increased production in China and India. Remarkably, despite the large increases in output, sugar prices have remained stable, rising modestly from $0.24 per pound in 1988 to $0.29 per pound by 1996. This price stability is attributable to the dramatic rise in the domestic consumption of sugar in the exporting nations. In fact, only 28.4 percent of total production was exported in 1997 (CRB *Commodity Yearbook*).

An examination of the stocks of raw sugar suggests that oversupply, which had been moderate through 1995, is now on the rise. The ratio of stocks to consumption for raw sugar is presented in Table 1.6. The rise in this ratio is due mainly to stockpiling by India, whose stores have increased by 4.8 million metric tons since 1988, so that by 1997 its holdings represented nearly one-third of the world stock. The reductions seen in Brazil, France, and Mexico could not offset India's rising inventories. The persistent oversupply of sugar is likely to place continued downward pressure on prices well into the future.

The International Cocoa Market

Cocoa production is largely confined to a handful of developing nations in Africa, South America, and Southeast Asia (Table 1.7). The numbers indicate two divergent trends in the concentration of cocoa production

Table 1.6

World Sugar Holdings, 1988–1997

Year	Ratio	Year	Ratio
1988	0.19	1993	0.19
1989	0.18	1994	0.16
1990	0.18	1995	0.18
1991	0.19	1996	0.21
1992	0.21	1997	0.22

Source: Foreign Agricultural Service, USDA.

Table 1.7

Cocoa Production, 1974 and 1997 (in thousands of metric tons and as a percentage of world output)

Key Producer	1974	(%)	1997	(%)
Brazil	246	17.0	198	7.4
Cameroon	110	7.6	110	4.1
Ghana	350	24.2	390	14.7
Indonesia	[1]	1.0	280	10.5
Ivory Coast	209	14.4	1,050	39.5
Malaysia	[1]	1.0	120	4.5
Nigeria	215	6.2	150	5.6

Source: Foreign Agricultural Service, USDA.
[1] Not a significant producer in that year.

in the period from 1974 to 1997. First, production expanded beyond Africa and South America into Southeast Asia, with Indonesia and Malaysia enjoying, respectively, 10.5 percent and 4.5 percent of world output. Second, the Ivory Coast nearly tripled its market share to command 39.5 percent of world production, thereby eclipsing Ghana as the dominant producer. At the same time, Brazil and Cameroon saw their market shares erode significantly. As a result of this reorientation of production, the proportion of exports due to the top four producers (concentration ratio) of cocoa stood at 72.1 percent in 1997, a significant rise over the ratio of 63.2 percent recorded in 1974. From these figures, one must conclude that the cocoa market is becoming increasingly oligopolistic.

The divergence between world output and demand suggests that the cocoa market is subject to almost permanent oversupply. In 1985, for example, 1.97 million metric tons of cocoa were produced, but only 1.84 million tons were absorbed by importing nations, this difference

Table 1.8

Excess Cocoa Production, 1981–1989 (as a percentage of world output)

Year	(%)	Year	(%)
1981	5.8	1986	6.5
1982	7.8	1987	1.8
1983	6.9	1988	9.8
1984	−13.3	1989	14.2
1985	11.0		

Source: Foreign Agricultural Service, USDA.

representing 11 percent of total output (Table 1.8). While the levels of overproduction were significantly less in other years, the accumulated effect by 1989 was an excess production of many thousands of metric tons. The trend was somewhat reversed between 1992 and 1994, when very small surpluses were produced. Significantly, in 1995 and 1997, total exports exceeded world output and thus the market was somewhat stabilized.

The International Petroleum Market

Although the world's major petroleum reserves are concentrated in the Middle East and North Africa, over the past twenty-five years countries with smaller deposits have increasingly affected the world market (Table 1.9). In 1974, world production was largely controlled by member nations of the Organization for Petroleum Exporting Countries (OPEC), but petroleum output is currently far too dispersed to be considered oligopolistic.

As will be argued in chapter 3, the most important measure of concentration for this market is the percentage of total production attributable to OPEC, a considerably higher number in 1974 than the standard four-firm concentration ratios usually employed to measure oligopoly power. This ratio is, in fact, what gave OPEC its power in the 1970s. By the late 1980s, however, the members of the cartel controlled a considerably smaller share of total output and exercised very little market control on petroleum prices.

CARTELS AND INTERNATIONAL TRADE

Beginning with the remarkable economic impact of OPEC in the 1970s, the interest in cartels as a means of determining commodity prices grew. Although OPEC's ability to control petroleum production and pricing seemingly ended nearly two decades ago, when the cartel joined its forces

Table 1.9

Petroleum Production, 1974 and 1997 (in thousands of barrels per day and as a percentage of world output)

Key Producer	1974	(%)	1997	(%)
Algeria	[1]	—	1,204	1.9
Canada	617	3.0	1,820	2.9
China	475	2.3	3,131	4.9
Libya	555	2.7	1,400	2.2
Iran	2,198	10.7	3,690	5.8
Kuwait	930	4.5	2,060	3.2
Nigeria	823	4.0	2,185	3.4
Mexico	238	1.2	2,851	4.5
Indonesia	502	2.4	1,545	2.4
Former USSR	3,374	16.4	—	—
Russia	[2]	—	5,866	9.2
Saudi Arabia	3,096	15.1	8,205	12.9
United Kingdom	[1]	—	2,550	4.0
United States	3,203	15.6	6,479	10.2
Venezuela	1,086	5.3	3,036	4.8

Source: Energy Information Administration.
Note: Numbers do not total 100 percent because only major producers are included.
[1] Not a major producer in that year.
[2] Russia's production for 1974 is included in the total for the USSR.

with Mexico and Norway to substantially tighten supplies in 1999, it once again demonstrated its power to manipulate the market. A similar supply situation—and the possibility of widespread controls—exists with other nonsubstitutable commodities utilized by industrialized nations. We will inevitably see higher prices, not only for commodities but also for industrial products that require these resources as inputs.

Despite the attractiveness of cartelization to producers, few markets actually conform to the conditions necessary for the successful operation of a cartel. Indeed, of the numerous collusive agreements formed since around the turn of the century, most have resulted in disappointment and disillusionment for the participants. The latter part of the chapter will examine the reasons cartels fail. Oftentimes, it is more advantageous for commodity exporters to avoid cartelization and seek alternative means of price stabilization.

The Objectives of Cartelization

The ultimate goal of cartels is to manipulate the world price of specific commodities. If the cartel raises world prices, the result will be a surplus of production and downward pressure on prices, a situation that can only be offset by permanently removing the excess supplies of the commodity. Such supply management, however, can exhaust the resources of the cartel. Consequently, the cartel members would be better served by limiting quantities at the point of production. In this way, the costs of curtailing output are absorbed by the individual cartel members, and the need to collect the monies necessary for stockpiling is eliminated.

Rather than seeking long-term price increases for their commodity, cartels should strive to smooth prices in order to prevent economic disruptions. Price instability is particularly problematic for developing nations, whose economies are often dependent on the export of a single product. In these cases, price fluctuations can result in recurring and destabilizing cycles of growth and recession.

Alternatively, the cartel may seek to actually raise the price of its commodity by fundamentally altering the market's structure. Frequently, the market for a given raw material is at least somewhat competitive in nature, and an uncoordinated attempt to raise prices simply results in a shift by the purchaser from one supplier to another. If, however, the cartel is able to fully coordinate production and pricing among its members, then it becomes possible to achieve a long-term price increase. Nonetheless, in nearly all instances, a certain number of commodity producers remain outside the collusive agreement and sell below the target price set by the cartel. Moreover, the price increases achieved by the cartel can encourage the search for substitutes or the implementation of conservation measures. Indeed, when OPEC pushed oil prices to a record annual price of $37 per barrel by 1980, the industrialized nations responded with widespread substitution and conservation initiatives that ultimately led to the collapse of the cartel's pricing power.

Whether the goal of cartelization is to raise prices or reduce price variability, cartel members must find a way to manage supply. This objective can be achieved through a number of mechanisms, each dependent upon the market characteristics for the given commodity. In the case of goods that can be stored for extended periods of time (e.g., rubber and tin), the cartel can purchase and retain significant quantities of its own commodity until market conditions improve. If the target price of the cartel is realistic, then the establishment of such buffer stocks can be an effective means of controlling both price fluctuations and supplies. As will be argued in chapter 3, however, if the price set by the cartel is too high (as it was for tin in the early 1980s), the association's funding will be exhausted and the producers will experience a rapid market collapse and severe economic dislocation. (For an examination of the various means of controlling prices, see Gilbert 1987.)

An alternative means of restricting total world production has been pursued by OPEC. In this instance, member nations are assigned an at-the-well production quota that eliminates the need for a buffer stock. Since funds do not have to be collected from cartel members for the purpose of purchasing excess supply, this arrangement has the decided advantage of reducing the costs of operating the cartel. The drawback of this system is the cartel's need to police its members to ensure that production quotas are respected. Indeed, the incidence of widespread over-production by certain OPEC members led to a breakdown in cooperation in the cartel in the mid-1980s.

A similar system of controls was instituted through the International Coffee Agreements (ICAs), which imposed restrictions on shipments. These arrangements, however, were complicated by the nature of coffee production, which is highly affected by weather conditions. Thus when unusually favorable climatic conditions result in coffee production above a nation's given quota, the producer may be forced to store the excess. While a season-to-season withholding of stocks is feasible, if the over-supply continues, the coffee may simply have to be destroyed.

A third, and truly unique, situation exists for the bauxite cartel. Beginning with the end of the colonial era, the developing nations that hold rich deposits of bauxite—including Guinea, Jamaica, and Suriname—essentially leased the rights to mine the compound to multinational corporations. In return for access to the raw rocky material, the firms hired some local labor and paid a per-ton levy back to the host country. Although the bauxite cartel was a loose organization, its members nonetheless worked in concert to force the international aluminum producers to raise their per-ton levies. The producers, in turn, either passed the increased cost of extracting bauxite onto consumers or simply absorbed the increase themselves. Thus the nations holding bauxite deposits received higher levies on the material without ever having to enter the market.

The Conditions of Successful Cartelization

Although a significant number of cartels have been formed since the 1970s, when international agencies such as UNCTAD actively promoted collusion, in most cases cartelization has proved to be an inappropriate means of stabilizing markets. The reason for this ineffectiveness is that very few cartels meet all of the criteria necessary for the successful management of output and prices. As a result, cartels have enjoyed only short-term elevation of prices, and most have eventually dissolved.

For a cartel to succeed, the commodity produced by its members must be homogeneous or easily differentiated into a limited number of product classes. Attempts to cartelize markets with very diversified product types will invariably result in complex price structures and internal conflict. An example of limited product categorization is the two-tier pricing structure devised by OPEC from its inception to differentiate between low-sulfur (sweet) and high-sulfur crude oil. Without this distinction, producers of low-sulfur oil could have argued that they were being undercompensated for a superior product. But it was equally important to limit the petroleum grades to only two classifications, for the establishment of additional quality categories would have entailed difficult negotiations that could have led to dissension among cartel members. Indeed, it can be said that OPEC's success in manipulating prices in the 1970s hinged on its recognition of only two grades of crude oil.

The problem of product heterogeneity has plagued the International Coffee Organization (ICO), the cartel founded to regulate coffee bean production and prices. In an attempt to simplify the pricing structure for the wide range of quality grades that its members produced, the ICO imposed a system whereby all coffee beans were designated as being either of the higher-quality arabica or the lower-grade robusta type. Yet even within this two-grade system, certain cartel members marketed their beans as being superior to other beans within the same classification. Recognizing the futility of managing such a large market, the ICO decided not to enforce its directives on producers of robusta coffee beans and instead maintained strict pricing and production guidelines for higher-quality beans only.

The successful cartelization of a market also requires that no direct substitutes for the product exist. After a long history of controlling production and pricing, the tin cartel collapsed in 1985 as a result of the substitution of other materials for tin in manufacturing processes. Had the cartel engineered an orderly retreat in prices, it could have protected the economies of its members, but instead it sought to maintain high target prices by adding to its buffer stock. As a result of these purchases, the tin cartel exhausted its funds and soon disintegrated.

As a counter example, OPEC reaped the benefits of the near nonsubstitutability of oil in the economies of the industrialized world, seeing a near 2,200 percent price increase between 1973 and 1978. Despite this extreme price escalation, the cartel managed to maintain market control only until 1985, when competition from non-OPEC producers, together with conservation efforts in the industrialized countries, sapped it of its economic power.

The successful management of both supply and price also requires that production be concentrated within a limited number of nations. Establishing quotas, a necessary condition for the stabilization of prices, is an extremely difficult process because it requires compromises from all cartel members. The larger the membership, the more contentious the negotiation process becomes and, as will be argued shortly, the stronger the temptation to violate the agreement. Specifically, once market prices have been increased, it is possible for members to generate additional revenues and profits through surreptitious price-cutting. The cartel's stability is threatened if cheating becomes widespread and the target price cannot be maintained. Consequently, it sometimes becomes necessary to institute internal policing measures to ensure that production quotas are being followed. Given the difficulty in uncovering quota violations when production is widely dispersed, the self-regulation process is problematic for even the smallest cartels and nearly impossible for large cartels (e.g., those of cocoa, with eight producing countries, and sugar, with eleven). The same would not hold true for the platinum industry should it seek cartelization, for 99 percent of world production takes place within only four countries. (For an analytical look at the role market structure plays in determining the relative success of cartels, see Fraas and Greer 1977.)

The fourth requirement for a workable collusive agreement is the existence of significant barriers to entry. Many cartel arrangements involve natural resources that occur in only a limited number of nations. Other cartels were established to manage the production of agricultural products—such as sugar, cocoa, and coffee—that can be grown wherever the climate is favorable. If the cartel is successful in raising prices in the long run, then new producers will be induced to enter the market. Unless these new suppliers enter into the collusive arrangement, prices will begin to soften and the cartel may collapse. Thus the markets for rare materials (e.g., bauxite, gold, platinum, tin, and tungsten) are far more conducive to cartelization than agricultural markets where free entry exists. The severe weakening of OPEC's power was largely the result of the entry of new non-OPEC suppliers, such as Mexico and China, into the market in response to higher petroleum prices. Indeed, OPEC's share of the world petroleum sales declined from a high of 73 percent in the early 1970s to less than 35 percent today. Consequently, the ability of the cartel to manipulate world prices has been significantly weakened.

Finally, the market for many commodities cannot be cartelized because of the nature of the product itself. In order to prevent the substitution that higher prices encourage, the cartel must be able to both restrict the supply of the commodity during periods of overproduction and increase the supply somewhat when production declines. Ideally, this management of supply is accomplished through stockpiling, a process that was utilized extensively under the now defunct International Tin Agreements. While it is possible to fine-tune output to meet the production goals of the cartel, the desired price is more easily achieved by manipulating the quantity of the product introduced into the market, but if the commodity under consideration is perishable, these market adjustments are infeasible. Thus while many agricultural products, such as coffee, sugar, and cocoa, can be stored for significant periods of time, other goods do not have a long shelf life. In addition, production levels cannot be adjusted once a planting cycle is under way unless the cartel members are willing to reduce supply by deliberately destroying the harvested product.

The Self-Defeating Tendencies of Cartelization

While cartelization is tremendously appealing to nations that depend on single-commodity exporting, the resulting market changes can ultimately defeat the objectives of the collusive arrangement. It is possible to design a market intervention that will smooth out cyclical variations in prices and provide a level of certainty to producers. Yet, instead, most collusive agreements seek higher prices, an action that inevitably results in a surplus of production and increased pressure on the cartel to absorb excess supply. The funds required to purchase a sufficient quantity of the product, however, are seldom available. As will be discussed in chapter 3, the burden of maintaining ample buffer stocks has been an incessant problem for the cocoa, rubber, sugar, and tin cartels. Even in the face of these market experiences, however, it is difficult for nations exporting a single commodity to accept the notion that achieving higher prices should not be the primary objective of cartelization.

The task of creating a long-lived, effective cartel is a complex one. A reasonable goal for cartels is to reduce price variability and engineer orderly price declines when warranted. Yet such modest goals are unlikely to solve the many trade problems that developing nations have experienced during the past half century. As will be discussed in subsequent chapters, there are measures that the commodity-exporting nations can take to reduce their vulnerability to price changes. Some of these mechanisms represent variations on the cartel concept that better address the proven weaknesses of market collusion.

The Pricing Strategies of Cartels

The attractiveness of cartels results primarily from the competitive aspects of commodity markets. These markets are characterized by:

- High price elasticity for the export of any one producer.
- Reliance of producing nations upon the export earnings from a single commodity.
- Low income elasticity of demand for commodities exported by developing nations (e.g., cocoa, coffee, and sugar).
- Overproduction resulting from the need for increased export earnings on the part of producers.
- Concentration of production in the developing world.

When all of these circumstances exist, the terms of trade will eventually move against the producing nations.

The models of oligopoly pricing illustrate the difficulties facing these producers. Presented with a fairly homogeneous product from each exporter, consuming nations tend to select a supplier based on price. In response to this likelihood, the exporting nation may cut its price in order to generate additional demand, knowing that an increase in sales will be achieved at the expense of the other producers. In turn, the other exporters will be forced to cut their prices as well, and thus all of the market players will see reduced profits.

This profit squeeze can be presented in the game theory framework (Figure 1.1). Nation A, a producer of a commodity product, is considering lowering its price to generate additional demand. As demonstrated in Panel 1,

Figure 1.1   **Incentive to Price-Cut in the Oligopoly Model**

Panel 1: Sales

Nation A

		Maintain prices	Reduce prices
	Maintain prices	Stable/Stable	Much higher/ Much lower
Nation B			
	Reduce prices	Much lower/ Much higher	Slightly higher/ Slightly higer

Panel 2: Profitability of Sales

Nation A

		Maintain prices	Reduce prices
	Maintain prices	Stable/Stable	Much higher/ Much lower
Nation B			
	Reduce prices	Much lower/ Much higher	Lower/Lower

the result is a significant increase in the sales of Nation A, at the expense of an alternative producer, Nation B. Faced with losing its market share, Nation B follows Nation A's price cut. The result for both nations is market equilibrium and a slight increase in sales brought about by increased demand. But as shown in Panel 2, both nations experience a decline in profits, the short-run result of unbridled competition in an oligopolistic market.

In the long term, however, following a period of destructive competition most oligopolistic markets settle into a period of tacit—if not open—cooperation. For an illustration of the patterns of pricing and competition within an oligopoly, one can consider the U.S. airline industry. During the 1980s, the major carriers experienced a prolonged period of intense competition and losses. The bankruptcies of Pan American Airlines and Eastern Airlines demonstrated the tremendous pressure that corporations faced in their scramble for market share. It was not uncommon for an airline to announce significant airfare reductions, sometimes below the per-passenger cost of providing a seat, only to have its competitors match the unprofitable price. By late 1980s, the management of the major carriers decided that competition on fares was a losing proposition. The industry has since settled into a period of price cooperation that has resulted in record profits.

The problem of price interdependency has also been played out internationally, particularly in the developing world, where efforts to increase market share have driven down export earnings for all producers. The better approach is for exporting nations to collude—either tacitly or openly—to achieve a higher price. In this regard, these commodity exporters have a clear advantage over corporations operating in industrialized countries, where laws prohibiting collusive arrangements are in place. The key disadvantage for the developing nations is the unpleasant effect of curtailing production for the sake of firming prices. Thus whereas U.S. domestic air carriers are able to reduce the negative effects of lower output through various means, such as leasing planes and altering service routes, a single-commodity exporting nation is under considerable pressure to continue producing and selling its product in order to secure foreign reserves. Consequently, even when global production substantially exceeds demand, little reduction in output occurs. The situation is even more complex for developing nations that export agricultural commodities, for it is impossible to establish a set production level for a given crop cycle and so the threat of substantial overproduction remains constant. For example, while cocoa, coffee, and even sugar can be stored temporarily in the hope that market conditions will improve, eventually the output must be either sold or destroyed. Consequently, nations that rely on agricultural exports are most vulnerable to the destabilizing effects of price erosion.

Despite its shortcomings, a formalized cartel arrangement can be superior to a simple tacit agreement on prices. In the past, the members of the various international cartels pledged, at least temporarily, to reduce output and restore some stability to their markets. Not surprisingly, many of these collusive arrangements were very short-lived, since the market for the commodity did not fulfill one or more of the conditions necessary for cartelization (as outlined above). For example, the substitution of tin with other compounds in manufacturing prevented the tin cartel from stabilizing prices. Even when a cartel meets all of the criteria for successful collusion (e.g., the agreements covering bauxite), there remains an inherent instability, as elevated prices encourage members to violate the accord in order to see even greater gains.

This instability can be easily demonstrated using demand and cost relationships for the individual cartel members. Nation i's cost function, $C(Q)$, is assumed to be increasing in Q and:

$C_i'\ (Q_i > 0$, marginal cost is greater than 0)

$C_i'\ (Q_i > 0$, marginal cost is increasing in Q)

P_{cartel} is the established cartel price. Once P_{cartel} is set, the revenue function of a member of the collusive agreement is:

$$P_{cartel} \times Q_i.$$

In order to maintain the cartel price, each member of the arrangement must be assigned a production quota. At this point, the cartel resembles a monopoly firm with multiple points of production. Thus, unlike nations that operate independently, the cartel as a whole faces a down-sloping monopoly curve.

The price increase achieved through collusion offers an even greater incentive for individual producers to cheat on the cartel. Nation i, after the establishment of the cartel, faces a revenue function equal to $R_i(Q)$. Presumably:

$$R_i{}'(Q_i) > 0, \text{ marginal revenue is positive}$$

$$R_i{}'(Q_i) < 0, \text{ marginal revenue is decreasing in } Q$$

If marginal revenue exceeds marginal cost, as one would assume under conditions of cartelization, then an expansion of output by a rogue cartel member will yield additional profits for that producer. If Nation i is initially assigned Q_c units of output under the cartel, but chooses to output Q_i, then total profits are:

$$P_{cartel} \times Q_c + R_i[Q_i - Q_c] - C(Q_c) - C(Q_i - Q_c)$$

Thus as long as the following exists

$$R_i[Q_i - Q_c] - C(Q_i - Q_c) > 0$$

then Nation i has an incentive to cheat. This condition will hold for as long as the cartel maintains a degree of monopoly power (alternatively, one could use the graphical model of collusion and the incentive to cheat available in standard microtheory texts). The stability of the cartel is immediately threatened if cheating by an individual member is uncovered.

The threat of nonconformity plagued OPEC from its inception. As OPEC forced the price of petroleum upward beginning in 1974 (from $3.14 per barrel to nearly $37 per barrel by 1980), cartel members were strongly tempted to exceed their quotas, especially since the cost of additional production was marginal while the potential revenues were so high. In the subsequent history of OPEC, numerous attempts were made to rein in production by the member nations who were violating their output ceilings. In a desperate attempt to demonstrate the corrosive effects of noncompliance, in 1986 Saudi Arabia began pumping petroleum at a rate well above its quota. For a brief period, the industrialized world enjoyed oil prices of $10 per barrel before the cartel members restored cooperation on production quotas.

SUMMARY AND CONCLUSION

The concentration of production of key commodities in the developing world has made cartels an attractive market strategy for exporting nations. Free from the legal constraints that prevented collusion in the industrialized countries and often dependent on the revenues from a single commodity, the developing nations seized on the chance to firm prices. As discussed above, the developing world's market share of commodities continues to increase as the role played by industrialized countries in world production diminishes. As reserves of critical materials dwindle, there may be a resurgence of cartelization. Yet future collusive agreements must address the fundamental instabilities that have undermined the success of cartels in the past.

It is intriguing to consider the experience of oligopolistic markets within Europe and the United States, for although forbidden from colluding, corporations there have achieved varying levels of tacit market cooperation. The result has been a significant increase in profitability. Whether a similar form of price stabilization could be secured in commodity markets is an open question. Certainly, some means of addressing overproduction must be found. Attempts to eradicate instability in the markets of the developing world must tackle the debilitating problem of economic dependence on single-commodity exporting.

REFERENCES

Commodity Research Bureau. Various dates. *The Commodity Yearbook.* New York: John Wiley and Sons.

Fraas, A., and Greer, D. 1977. "Market Structure and Price Collusion: An Empirical Analysis." *Journal of Industrial Economics* 26, no. 1: 21–44.

Gilbert, C. 1987. "International Commodity Agreements: Design and Performance." *World Development* 15, no. 5: 591–616.

2

The Dependence of Developing Nations on Commodity Exports

As discussed in chapter 1, production of most key commodities is centered in the developing world. In many cases, the exported goods constitute a significant proportion of the country's foreign earnings, and therefore price variability in commodity markets can result in severe economic stress. As commodity prices slide, the funds needed to procure the imports critical for development decrease. The result is falling growth rates, the inability to repay international financial obligations, and potential political instability.

This chapter will consider the relative dependency of developing nations on single- versus multiple-export trading. The numbers show that the impact of price instability is most severe for single-commodity exporters. Thus Ghana, which relies almost entirely on cocoa to secure foreign exchange, is far more vulnerable to price swings than a diversified exporter like Brazil. Although prices of primary commodities have tended to move in tandem, rising in the 1970s and falling together in the 1980s, this price correlation is not absolute. It is unlikely, for example, that the international markets for cocoa, coffee, sugar, and tin—all significant exports of Brazil—will simultaneously see a decline in prices. It appears that a broadly diversified export mix spreads out the risk of falling prices. By estimating the impact that declining commodity prices have exerted on export earnings during the last two decades, it becomes clear that even modest changes in a nation's product mix can result in significant economic benefits.

The chapter concludes with an examination of UNCTAD, the first global commission to aggressively support the formation of "cooperative" cartels (i.e., those that incorporate both producing and consuming nations). The discussion of UNCTAD's efforts to empower developing nations by fostering the concept of cartelization will serve as a springboard to the overview of individual cartels presented in chapter 3.

SOURCES OF INSTABILITY IN PRIMARY COMMODITY MARKETS

While advocates of cartelization attribute commodity price instability primarily to supply-side fluctuations, variations in demand also play a significant role. This is particularly true for the raw materials exported from developing nations for use in manufacturing processes in the industrialized world. During recessionary periods, demand for these intermediate inputs declines and commodity prices usually fall. This is the situation that faces exporters of bauxite, rubber, tin, and—somewhat less so—petroleum, for none of these products are destined for final consumption. Conversely, the markets for cocoa, coffee, and sugar are somewhat less affected by recessionary periods, since demand is not dependent on the level of industrial output. This helps explain the very low income elasticity of demand for these latter commodities.

Chu and Morrison (1986) empirically tested the importance of shifts in supply and demand on commodity prices for the period from 1969 to 1982. Their analysis suggested that prices for food crops are influenced by both the level of manufacturing output in the developed world (demand) and the level of production (supply). Prices of industrial raw materials such as bauxite, rubber, and tin, on the other hand, were shown to be primarily determined by demand. In contrast, in an earlier study, Hwa (1979) had emphasized the importance of both supply and stockpiles on commodity prices; he determined that both production and carryover stocks resulted in lower prices for industrial commodities.

The relationship between economic growth in the developed world and commodity prices is easily demonstrated. During the recession experienced by the industrialized nations from 1991 to 1992, for instance, the price of most major commodities declined significantly. By 1993, petroleum, aluminum, and tin prices had fallen by 13.0 percent, 12.6 percent, and 7.7 percent, respectively (Table 2.1). Rubber prices, on the other hand, remained remarkably stable, declining only 1.5 percent over the same period. The prices of the agricultural commodities of coffee, cocoa, and sugar fell by 15.3 percent, 6.5 percent, and 2.1 percent, respectively. Although the rather significant fall in coffee prices biases the

Table 2.1

Change in Prices for Key Commodities, 1991–1993 and 1993–1994
(as percentages)

Commodity	Change, 1991–1993	Change, 1993–1994
Coffee	−15.3	83.2
Cocoa	−6.5	25.8
Sugar	−2.1	13.2
Aluminum	−12.6	29.4
Petroleum	−13.0	−5.5
Rubber	−1.5	32.6
Tin	−7.7	5.7

Source: CRB, *Commodity Yearbook.*

figures, the average price decline for the agricultural products was some-what less (8.0 percent) than that for the industrial inputs (8.7 percent). Similarly, price recovery was less rapid in the tin, petroleum, rubber, and aluminum markets. Although prices in the latter two markets had risen significantly by 1994, the tin and petroleum markets remained weak, and oil prices actually continued to fall. The observed price trends for aluminum, rubber, and tin are consistent with the findings presented by Chu and Morrison. The lower magnitude of the price reductions in the cocoa and sugar markets is to be expected given the presumed domi-nance of supply-side effects in agricultural markets.

The Undiversified Commodity Exporters and Price Variability

Ghana: The Price Paid for Its Dependence on Cocoa

The economic dislocations that arise from single-commodity exporting are perhaps best symbolized by the experiences of Ghana. Of the 2.7 million metric tons of cocoa produced worldwide during the 1996–1997 growing season, Ghana was responsible for nearly 15 percent (390,000 metric tons). Only the Ivory Coast, with nearly 40 percent of world out-put, contributes more to total production. Unlike other major producers of cocoa such as Brazil, Indonesia, Malaysia, and Nigeria, Ghana does not have a secondary commodity to rely on for earnings when cocoa prices are in decline.

The percentages of Ghana's foreign exchange earnings from cocoa ex-ports for the years from 1974 to 1980 and from 1990 to 1997 are shown in

Table 2.2

Ghana's Export Earnings from Cocoa, 1974–1980 and 1990–1996
(in millions of dollars and as a percentage of total exports)

Year	($)	(%)
1975	801	59.3
1976	779	53.9
1977	890	58.3
1978	893	60.1
1979	1,066	67.4
1980	1,104	74.1
1990	319	35.5
1991	306	30.7
1992	241	24.4
1993	305	28.7
1994	384	31.0
1995	419	29.3
1996	568	36.2

Source: IMF, *International Financial Statistics*, and CRB, *Commodity Yearbook.*

Table 2.2. The figures from the 1970s demonstrate Ghana's dependence on cocoa exports during the cartel era. With prices rising throughout that decade, the percentage of exports attributable to cocoa continued to increase, exceeding 74 percent in 1980. In subsequent years, the cocoa market weakened, and Ghana attempted, with only limited success, to expand its export base. In 1990, over 46 percent of Ghana's total export earnings were still attributable to cocoa. This figure fell as low as 24.4 percent in 1993, and yet the metric tons of cocoa exported had actually risen by over 28 percent between 1992 and 1993. The reduced importance of cocoa in Ghana's export structure was simply a reflection of a collapsing market, for cocoa prices had plummeted to $978 per metric ton by 1993, their lowest level since 1974. When cocoa prices recovered to $1,409 per metric ton in 1996, Ghana's export earnings for the commodity rose to over one-third of total exports.

The difficulty facing developing nations like Ghana, whose export earnings are largely dependent on single-commodity trade, can be demonstrated by altering the earnings figures to reflect a fixed export price for cocoa equal to the average for the nine years in question. Although cocoa prices varied from a high of $1,599 per metric ton in 1988 to a low of $978 per metric ton in 1993, the average price was $1,213 per metric ton. If prices had been fixed, then even during the leanest years, Ghana's export earnings from cocoa would have been $357.8 million in 1990 (12.3 percent higher than the actual figure), $355.4 million in 1991 (16.0 percent higher), $294.8 million in 1992 (22.6 percent higher), and $378.5 million

Table 2.3

Saudi Arabia's Export Earnings from Petroleum, 1975–1985 and 1990–1996 (in billions of dollars and as a percentage of total exports)

Year	(b$)	(%)
1975	27.38	100.0
1976	36.13	100.0
1977	42.24	100.0
1978	39.24	91.9
1979	101.66	92.4
1980	132.54	93.0
1981	126.35	93.0
1982	76.79	92.6
1983	55.06	93.3
1984	48.61	91.3
1985	33.77	—
1990	53.74	90.3
1991	57.25	91.3
1992	57.87	92.5
1993	50.33	91.1
1994	47.28	89.0
1995	51.55	—
1996	61.15	—

Source: IMF, *International Financial Statistics*.

in 1993 (24.0 percent higher). Clearly, the economic status of the country would have been substantially improved if prices had remained stable during this period.

The impact of price variability on Ghana's economy can be seen by examining figures for its gross domestic product during the downturn in the cocoa market. Real economic growth in Ghana, which averaged 4.7 percent for the period from 1987 to 1993, fell to 3.8 percent in 1994 (source: International Monetary Fund, 1998). By 1995, with cocoa prices recovering, economic growth rose 4.5 percent. Although some diversification of Ghana's export structure has taken place, the nation's economy remains very sensitive to conditions in the international cocoa market.

OPEC: Power with Dependence

The history of OPEC provides perhaps the best illustration of the pitfalls of relying on single-commodity trade. Even though the member states of Ecuador, Iran, and Nigeria have achieved a degree of export diversification since the 1970s, others such as Saudi Arabia and Venezuela have remained almost wholly dependent on earnings from petroleum production. With real petroleum prices reaching historic lows in 1998, economic conditions in the latter nations worsened.

Table 2.4

Venezuela's Export Earnings from Petroleum, 1974–1985 and 1990–1997
(in billions of dollars and as a percentage of total exports)

Year	(b$)	(%)
1974	10.5	93.8
1975	8.3	94.5
1976	8.8	94.2
1977	9.1	94.8
1978	8.7	95.1
1979	13.6	95.1
1980	17.6	91.7
1981	18.6	88.6
1982	15.6	94.0
1983	13.9	99.7
1984	14.8	92.7
1985	13.0	90.3
1990	14.0	79.7
1991	15.2	—
1992	11.2	79.0

Table 2.3 details the export structure of Saudi Arabia from 1988 to 1995.[1] With petroleum representing approximately 90 percent of its total exports, Saudi Arabia's economy is vulnerable to the vagaries of wildly fluctuating prices. Indeed, prices dipped as low as $14.72 per barrel in 1988 and as high as $22.97 per barrel in 1990, when Saudi Arabia's real GDP rose by 10.7 percent. Oil prices then began a steady decline, reaching $15.90 per barrel in 1994, with the growth rate in GDP correspondingly falling to just 0.5 percent. Even with the recent resurgence of petroleum prices from their near-historic lows of December 1998, the near-term prospects of the Saudi economy appear bleak.

The situation is quite similar in Venezuela, where in 1974 petroleum accounted for nearly 94 percent of exports (Table 2.4). As oil prices accelerated in the late 1970s, this percentage rose to over 95 percent. Despite falling prices, the degree of Venezuela's dependence on petroleum exports remained high during the 1980s. By 1990, the country had made minimal progress in diversifying its trade structure, with approximately 80 percent of export earnings attributable to oil. This percentage continued to drop to just 68.3 percent in 1994, but by 1997 it had returned to its 1990 level. Consequently, Venezuela remains economically vulnerable to conditions in the petroleum markets. Figure 2.1, which compares

Figure 2.1 **Petroleum Exports as a Percentage of Total Exports, 1974–1997**

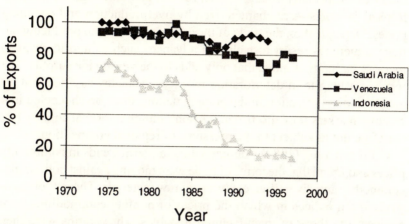

the relative dependence of Saudi Arabia and Venezuela on petroleum exports with that of the less oil-dependent OPEC member, Indonesia, will be considered below.

The growth rate of real GDP in Venezuela averaged 2.75 percent during the period from 1987 to 1997, a level commensurate with other Latin American nations. The drop in the average price of petroleum in 1988—from $18.15 to $14.72 per barrel—resulted in a reversal of Venezuela's economic expansion, with the growth rate of GDP declining by –7.8 percent in 1989. A recovery took place in 1990, when oil prices rose to $22.97 per barrel, with the country's real GDP rising by 6.9 percent that year and by another 9.7 percent in 1991. But by 1994, prices had sunk again and the nation's economy shrank by 2.3 percent. With only feeble attempts to diversify its foreign trade, Venezuela remains extremely vulnerable to swings in the petroleum market.

A similar dependence on petroleum exports could be demonstrated for nearly every member of OPEC. The willingness of most oil-exporting nations to join the cartel and remain members even during periods when OPEC exerts no significant control over the market bespeaks an overreliance on petroleum earnings.

The More Diversified Commodity Exporters and Price Variability

Although significant benefits may arise when developing nations are able to diversify their exports, some authors have argued that, diversified or not, dependence on commodity trade is detrimental to a nation's economic health. Madeley (1993) noted that the markets for most commodities—especially cocoa, coffee, rubber, and other agricultural and tropical products—are characterized by overproduction and declining prices. Dependent on the trade of these commodities, the producing nations sometimes resort to technical advances such as hybrid crops to increase earnings, a move that only adds to the worldwide surplus. The result is a long-term deterioration in prices. Madeley asserted that attempts at diversification in developing nations must be channeled into creating markets for exports that are nontraditional for that country and therefore not as subject to the pressures of regional competition.

Grilli and Yang (1988) examined the long-term trends in commodity prices and found that the terms of trade were moving against both single-commodity and diversified exporters of raw materials. The authors constructed ten indices in which the prices of nonfuel commodities were compared to those of manufactured tradables. These ratios were then regressed against a time trend for the years 1900 through 1986. Regardless of the index used, the numbers revealed a significant deterioration in relative prices over this period. Grilli and Yang then conducted similar estimations for individual commodity groups under such classifications as food, metals, and cereals. In only one instance—tropical fruits—was an improvement in the terms of trade uncovered. The authors noted that a variety of explanations exist for the declining terms of trade, within both the neoclassical models and the Prebisch-Singer framework. Regardless of the specific source of declining terms of trade, the implications of export diversification for developing nations were unilaterally unfavorable. The work of Grilli and Yang suggests that although diversifying commodity trade yields considerable benefit in the short run, it does not provide long-term protection to exporting nations.

Similarly, Diakosavvas and Scandizzo (1991) conducted empirical tests on the relative prices of commodities versus those for manufactured goods for the period from 1900 to 1982 and found declining terms of trade for the commodity exporters. The authors concluded that there are several factors that cause alterations in the terms of trade, namely, chronic overproduction and excess supply of labor in developing nations, and technological changes and protectionism in the industrialized world. That their results do not hold for all commodities suggests that developing nations that export certain products may have benefited from changes in relative prices. The authors also noted that, with few exceptions, the relationship between individual commodity prices and a time trend is statistically weak. Although not rejecting the argument that prices have moved against de-

Table 2.5

Colombia's Export Earnings from Coffee, 1974–1980 and 1990–1996 (in millions of dollars and as a percentage of total exports)

Year	(m$)	(%)
1974	642.5	43.0
1975	797.0	47.4
1976	1,468.3	66.7
1977	2,519.3	94.7
1978	2,322.8	73.6
1979	2,655.8	77.2
1980	2,784.3	70.0
1990	1,358.0	19.2
1991	1,445.7	19.3
1992	1,392.7	19.2
1993	1,296.5	17.5
1994	1,689.7	19.3
1995	2,497.5	24.4
1996	1,984.7	18.6

Source: IMF, *International Financial Statistics*, and CRB, *Commodity Yearbook.*
Note: Numbers are approximate and based on "exportable" production (i.e., total output less domestic consumption).

veloping nations during the twentieth century, Diakosavvas and Scandizzo argued that the impact of declining commodity prices has not been as significant as sometimes asserted in the literature.

The empirical studies cited here made a strong case against developing nations diversifying their exports by producing and trading yet another commodity. Lacking the technology required to initiate production of even small-scale manufactures, however, many emerging nations have little choice but to focus on the trading of other commodities. The fact that a number of developing nations with relatively larger and more robust economies have broken their dependence on commodity trade and have experienced higher and less volatile economic growth does not negate the difficulties that face struggling commodity-producing nations.

Colombia and Coffee Exports

There can be marginal benefits gained from diversification into multiple commodities. This is the case with Colombia, which formerly relied on coffee for the majority of its export earnings (as late as 1983, it accounted for fully two-thirds of the country's exports). The importance of coffee in Colombia's trade has since declined substantially, averaging only 20 percent of exports in the 1990s (Table 2.5). As a result, the

Table 2.6

The Ivory Coast's Export Earnings from Coffee and Cocoa, 1975–1981 and 1990–1996 (in millions of dollars and as a percentage of total exports)

Year	Coffee (m$)	Coffee (%)	Cocoa (m$)	Cocoa (%)
1975	477.3	38.5	279.9	22.6
1976	1,561.3	—	459.8	26.5
1977	1,524.9	63.2	747.6	31.0
1978	820.8	31.4	935.1	35.7
1979	1,101.8	40.5	602.7	22.1
1980	1,030.0	34.2	909.4	30.2
1981	890.8	36.6	1,043.6	42.8
1990	553.2	19.0	784.2	26.9
1991	366.2	13.5	888.1	32.8
1992	330.0	11.2	806.4	27.4
1993	233.8	9.3	719.4	28.6
1994	463.0	16.5	1,154.4	41.1
1995	790.1	20.7	1,220.9	32.0
1996	493.4	11.3	1,649.8	37.7

Source: IMF, *International Financial Statistics*, and CRB, *Commodity Yearbook.*

nation's economy is no longer as susceptible to erratic swings in international coffee prices.

The Ivory Coast: Dual Dependence on Cocoa and Coffee

The trade reorientation of the Ivory Coast took a different turn. Although one of Africa's economic success stories, the Ivory Coast has always been heavily dependent on cocoa and coffee exports. In 1975, for example, these commodities made up over 60 percent of its exports and thus the country was highly vulnerable to price instabilities (Table 2.6). Gradually, the reliance on the trade of coffee has been reduced so that by 1996 the commodity was responsible for only 11.3 percent of total exports. At the same time that coffee exports were declining in importance, the Ivory Coast was promoting cocoa in its foreign trade. In 1995, cocoa represented only 22.6 percent of total exports, but by 1996, the figure stood at 37.7 percent. (Figure 2.2 illustrates the shift in the relative dependence of the Ivory Coast and Ghana on cocoa exports, with the former becoming much more reliant on this product.) Given the volatility of cocoa prices, it becomes clear that in shifting the importance of trade from coffee to cocoa, the Ivory Coast has not effectively shielded itself from market instabilities.

Figure 2.2 **Percentage of Exports Due to Cocoa, Ghana and the Ivory Coast, 1974–1997**

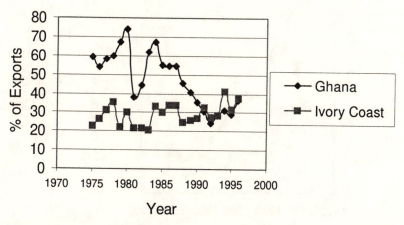

Unfortunately for the Ivory Coast, Colombia, and other coffee producers, prices in 1989 stood at $141.20 per 60 kilogram bag—the lowest price since 1975—and continued to slide until 1992, bottoming out at $84.00 per bag. Despite the weakness in the market and contrary to expectations, Colombia's output rose 4 percent in 1992 and 5.4 percent in 1993. Prices recovered rapidly, rising 154.8 percent from 1992 to 1995. Surprisingly, the Colombian economy did not respond in any significant way to these price changes, with the average growth of GDP for the period from 1989 to 1996 standing at just over 4 percent. The numbers therefore indicate that the diversification of Colombia's export base away from commodity trade has provided a significant degree of protection. Figure 2.3 provides a comparison of the situations that face Colombia and the Ivory Coast.

Bolivia and the Trade of Tin and Zinc

A somewhat unique situation exists for Bolivia, which has gradually ended its reliance on the export of one commodity, tin, only to become dependent on another, zinc. In 1972, the sale of tin represented 56.4 percent of the country's export earnings (Table 2.7). The tin market experienced significant turbulence in the 1970s and 1980s. When prices rose by nearly 144 percent from $6,862 per metric ton in 1975 to $16,743 per metric ton in 1980 (CRB *Commodity Yearbook*), Bolivia's economy surged. A gentle erosion in the market ensued, with the price of tin

Figure 2.3   **Coffee Exports as a Percentage of Total, Ivory Coast and Colombia, 1974–1996**

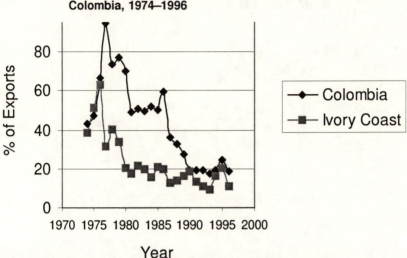

falling to $11,514 in 1985, just prior to the collapse of the International Tin Agreement in that year. By 1993, prices had plunged to a low of $5,156.8 per metric ton.

The numbers show that as the price of tin began to fall, Bolivia sought more stable revenues by gradually diversifying its economy into other tradables, particularly zinc. Indeed, the percentage of exports from the sale of tin stood at 29.9 percent in 1985, roughly one-half what it had been in 1972, and the fallout from the bankruptcy of the tin cartel in 1985 is reflected in the totals for 1986, which stood at just 16.2 percent. By 1997, with tin accounting for a mere 7.8 percent of tradables, the commodity had ceased to play a major role in the Bolivian economy. The proof that declining prices were responsible for the diminishing role of tin in the country's economy is evidenced by the fact that the physical volume of tin exports peaked in 1977 and fell nearly 46 percent by 1986 (CRB *Commodity Yearbook*). With the exception of a small dip from 1987 through 1988, the number of metric tons of tin exported has remained stable, falling by less than 7 percent between 1986 and 1997.

With Bolivia relying less on tin for its trade revenues, zinc began to play a larger role in the nation's economy. In 1972, zinc represented only 7.7 percent of exports (about the same level of importance that tin has now). Between 1972 and 1986, zinc exports actually declined in significance, falling to only 4.4 percent of total exports ($28 million). From 1988 onward, however, foreign sales rose sharply, and by 1989, zinc had

Table 2.7

Bolivia's Export Earnings from Tin and Zinc, 1972–1997 (in millions of dollars and as a percentage of total exports)

Year	Tin (m$)	Tin (%)	Zinc (m$)	Zinc (%)
1972	113.5	56.4	15.4	7.7
1973	131.0	50.3	26.0	10.0
1974	230.1	41.3	37.7	6.8
1975	171.4	38.6	40.3	6.8
1976	216.3	38.1	39.1	6.9
1977	328.8	52.1	44.7	7.1
1978	374.2	59.5	31.5	5.0
1979	395.6	52.1	42.7	5.6
1980	378.2	40.1	36.7	4.8
1981	343.1	37.6	40.4	4.4
1982	278.4	33.7	38.4	4.6
1983	207.9	27.5	33.4	4.4
1984	247.8	34.2	37.3	5.1
1985	186.7	29.9	29.5	4.7
1986	103.3	16.2	28.0	4.4
1987	68.9	12.1	32.7	5.7
1988	76.9	12.8	60.2	10.0
1989	126.5	15.4	132.2	16.1
1990	106.5	11.5	146.0	15.8
1991	99.7	11.7	139.7	16.5
1992	107.3	15.1	173.0	24.4
1993	83.3	11.5	119.5	16.4
1994	91.1	8.8	105.3	10.2
1995	88.6	8.0	151.3	13.8
1996	85.5	7.5	153.4	13.9
1997	88.4	7.8	198.8	17.6

Source: IMF, *International Financial Statistics.*

supplanted tin as Bolivia's key commodity export. In 1997, zinc sales stood at 17.6 percent of exports. Although this percentage is far less than the peak figure for tin exports (56.4 percent in 1972), Bolivia should still be concerned about its dependence on zinc for trade revenues.

The variations in tin prices have had an impact on the economic growth of Bolivia. The most notable price elevations for tin occurred in the 1970s, with annual increases of 42.4 percent (1976–1977), 15.8 percent (1977–1978), and 20.0 percent (1978–1979; see the CRB *Commodity Yearbook*). At the same time, Bolivia's real GDP rose 4.2 percent in 1977 and 3.4 percent in 1978, but only 1.8 percent in 1979. Major price declines occurred between 1980 and 1981, with prices retreating 15.6 percent, and between 1985 and 1986, with a decline of nearly 47 per-

Table 2.8

Correlations Between Commodity Prices and Economic Growth of Various Countries

Nation	Commodity	Period	Correlation
Ghana	Cocoa	1974–1986	0.506
		1987–1996	−0.739
Venezuela	Petroleum	1974–1985	0.553
		1986–1996	0.203
Saudi Arabia	Petroleum	1974–1985	0.890
		1986–1996	0.243
Indonesia	Petroleum	1974–1984	0.802
		1985–1996	0.243
Malaysia	Rubber	1974–1980	0.951
		1981–1996	0.302
Bolivia	Tin	1972–1982	0.931
		1983–1996	−0.564
Ivory Coast	Coffee	1974–1996	0.518
Colombia	Coffee	1974–1982	0.317
		1983–1996	−0.224

cent. As a result, the real GDP rose less than 1.0 percent in 1981, then fell by nearly 4.4 percent in 1982 and by 2.5 percent in 1986, and then increased by a modest 2.6 percent in 1987. These gentle but nonetheless persistent market movements suggest that although the Bolivian economy is less vulnerable to export price variations than other economies in the developing world, the market sensitivity remains measurable.

ESTIMATING THE LINK BETWEEN COMMODITY PRICES AND ECONOMIC GROWTH

The numbers above suggest an apparent link between commodity prices and growth in exporting nations. It is possible, however, to prove this relationship by estimating and then comparing the correlation between real GDP and prices for both single-commodity and diversified exporters. Special consideration will be given to nations (for example, the Ivory Coast, Colombia, Venezuela, and Malaysia) that previously exported a single product but now engage in a more complex trade structure. This latter analysis will establish whether diversification has reduced the impact of commodity market fluctuations on real gross domestic product.

The correlations between the price of key commodity exports and real GDP of various nations are shown in Table 2.8. Two correlations are presented, the first for periods of high and sustained dependence on a single export, and the second derived from the GDP and prices after diversification of each nation's export mix (the exception is the Ivory Coast, which remains heavily dependent on both coffee and cocoa sales).[2] The figures demonstrate that the relationship between economic growth and commodity prices apparent in the earlier period became weak or nonexistent for most of the nations after the era of collusive agreements ended in the early 1980s.

Given its past reliance on cocoa for the bulk of its international trade, Ghana could once have been considered a classic example of a single-commodity exporter. As shown in Table 2.2, cocoa accounted for nearly 75 percent of Ghana's foreign sales in 1980, but shortly thereafter dependence on sales of the commodity waned, and by 1992 it represented only 25 percent of total exports. Recently, this trend has been reversed, with cocoa's importance to Ghana's trade rising once again (comprising 36 percent of foreign sales in 1996). Even this latter figure suggests, however, that Ghana has made considerable progress in diversifying its trade beyond cocoa.

The correlation between cocoa prices and real GDP stood at 0.506 for the period from 1974 to 1986, prior to the diversification of trade. The link between the strength of the cocoa market and economic growth in Ghana was broken after 1986, when prices were no longer correlated with the gross domestic product. Thus, while cocoa remains a major tradable for Ghana, its price no longer drives the nation's growth.

The trade picture is somewhat less comforting for nondiversified petroleum exporters such as Saudi Arabia and Venezuela (Tables 2.3 and 2.4). For the former, oil has almost always comprised over 90 percent of total exports, leaving the country's economy vulnerable to even small market changes. Conversely, Venezuela has significantly reduced the proportion of export earnings attributable to petroleum from 95 percent in 1978 and 1979 to 78.7 percent in 1997. The correlation between Venezuela's output and the price of petroleum was 0.553 during the period from 1974 to 1985 and 0.168 for the years 1986 through 1996. This low correlation demonstrates that despite its high reliance on a single export, Venezuela has managed to protect itself somewhat from variations in oil prices. The correlations for Saudi Arabia are understandably higher, and yet a correlation of GDP with prices of only 0.243 for the period from 1986 to 1996 indicates that prices have only moderately affected economic growth.

The continued linkage of export prices to economic growth—even

Table 2.9

Indonesia's Export Earnings from Petroleum, 1974–1985 and 1990–1997
(in billions of dollars and as a percentage of total exports)

Year	(b$)	(%)
1974	5.21	70.2
1975	5.31	74.8
1976	6.00	70.2
1977	7.30	67.2
1978	7.44	63.9
1979	8.87	56.9
1980	12.85	58.7
1981	14.39	57.2
1982	14.36	64.3
1983	13.48	63.7
1984	12.10	55.3
1985	7.67	41.3
1990	6.48	25.2
1991	5.75	19.7
1992	5.85	17.2
1993	5.01	13.6
1994	6.01	15.0
1995	6.44	14.2
1996	7.24	14.6
1997	6.82	12.8

Source: IMF, *International Financial Statistics.*

if considerably weaker than it once was—helps explain the continued existence of OPEC. In March 1999, at a time when oil prices were in decline, OPEC once again closed ranks and agreed to significant cuts in production in order to firm prices. Although the organization has experienced problems in implementing its agreement, the fact that the cartel is still in existence is remarkable, particularly when one considers that some of its member states have successfully diversified their trade bases.

Indonesia provides a case in point, for although it relied on petroleum for over 55 percent of its exports in 1984, by 1997 oil revenues accounted for only 12.8 percent of foreign sales (Table 2.9). The primary benefit from this reorientation of trade has been the insulation of the Indonesian economy from cyclical downturns in the petroleum market. Indeed, the diminishing importance of petroleum to the country's trade is demonstrated by the fact that although steep declines in oil prices resulted in a drop in the growth of GDP from 7.0 percent in 1985 to 2.4 percent in 1986, price increases in 1990 and 1996 did not elevate the rate of economic growth. Until the destabilizing aftermath of the currency crisis of 1998, Indonesia was in the enviable position of experiencing sustained growth of 6 percent per year with no recessionary periods.

Although other OPEC members such as Iran, Saudi Arabia, the United Arab Emirates, and Venezuela remain almost entirely dependent on petroleum exports, Indonesia has managed to protect itself from price volatility. It should be noted that although the volume of petroleum shipped from Indonesia has dropped by 25 percent since 1981, export revenues have fallen by an astounding 53 percent. Therefore, it is not the case that the country's oil reserves are depleted, but rather that the export structure has been altered to a significant degree. Despite the ever-widening nature of its trade base, Indonesia will most likely maintain its membership in OPEC as yet another means of increasing export revenues.

Malaysia has traditionally played a significant role in a number of commodity markets, especially those for tin and rubber. At a time when the Malaysian economy was heavily dependent on export earnings from these two products—they accounted for 43 percent of total exports in 1974—interest in cartels was high (Table 2.10 and Figure 2.4). By 1980, this dependence had fallen to just 25.3 percent and, with further diversification, it could be said that by 1990 tin and rubber were no longer a vital source of foreign exchange for Malaysia (only 4.9 percent of exports).

Not surprisingly, Malaysia's economic growth in the 1990s was unaffected by price swings in the tin and rubber markets. Given the reorientation of its trade, the country has little to gain from collusive agreements that involve such a small percentage of total trade. Such diversification of exports represents a significant challenge to supporters of cartels, whose attempts to negotiate collusive agreements will undoubtedly be more difficult in the years to come.

DIVERSIFICATION OF EXPORTS

The analysis presented above demonstrates that developing nations make themselves susceptible to the adverse effects of market fluctuations when they become dependent on single-commodity trade for their export earnings. Clearly, there is an observable link between export prices and economic growth in nations such as the Ivory Coast, Saudi Arabia, and

Table 2.10

Malaysia's Export Earnings from Tin and Rubber, 1974–1980 and 1990–1997 (as a percentage of total exports)

Year	Tin (%)	Rubber (%)
1974	14.9	28.3
1975	13.1	21.9
1976	11.4	23.2
1977	11.4	22.6
1978	11.8	21.1
1979	9.6	18.5
1980	8.9	16.4
1990	1.1	3.8
1991	0.7	2.8
1992	0.7	2.3
1993	0.4	1.8
1994	0.3	1.9
1995	0.3	2.2
1996	0.3	1.8
1997	0.2	1.3

Source: IMF, *International Financial Statistics.*

Venezuela. In contrast, more diversified exporters such as Colombia and Malaysia are somewhat safeguarded against price instabilities and therefore their long-term growth potential is far more promising.

The benefits from diversification depend on the degree of co-variation between the prices of various commodities. For example, if the price of coffee and cocoa are closely correlated, then the Ivory Coast gains little by producing and exporting both products. Conversely, if the correlation in prices is low, then the economic growth of the nation will be largely shielded from instability in any single commodity market.

Table 2.11 illustrates the correlations between the prices of the seven commodities that are emphasized in this study. Of the twenty-one combinations possible, only four exhibit correlations that are sufficiently high to eliminate the benefits of diversification: coffee and cocoa, tin and petroleum, tin and cocoa, and bauxite and rubber. In two other instances—tin and coffee, and rubber and petroleum—the correlations are significant but not particularly high. These figures suggest that developing nations that rely on a single commodity could partially stabilize their export earnings by simply diversifying into an appropriate second product. Further diversification would provide additional benefits in terms of market stability.

Figure 2.4   **Tin and Rubber as a Percentage of Malaysia's Total Exports, 1974–1997**

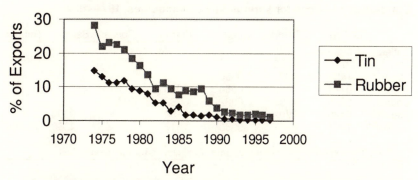

A more precise way of examining these trade advantages would be to compare the variation in prices facing both diversified and nondiversified commodity exporters. Table 2.12 presents the coefficient of variations of prices for the seven chosen commodities for the period from 1974 to 1996 versus that for five potential export combinations: rubber and coffee, tin and rubber, sugar and cocoa, rubber and cocoa, and coffee and cocoa. The relative volatility of the cocoa, sugar, and tin markets stands in contrast to the erratic prices for bauxite, coffee, and rubber. It is exporters of the former products that would most benefit from export diversification.

The low correlation between rubber and coffee prices suggests that coffee exporters would benefit from expanding trade to include rubber (Table 2.12). The coefficient of variation for prices falls from 0.331 for coffee alone to 0.276 for coffee and rubber combined. Similarly, tin exporters would experience a decline in the coefficient of variation of prices from 0.386 to 0.352 if rubber were also exported. The most intriguing example is that of sugar and cocoa, two products with remarkably high price variability, for the coefficient of variation of prices drops to 0.352 when both products are traded. This analysis demonstrates the advantages that accrue to nations that manage to diversify the structure of their exports.

The difficulty is that diversification is dependent on the endowments of the exporting nation. The rubber and cocoa, rubber and coffee, and cocoa and coffee combinations are certainly feasible given the similar climatic requirements of these crops. Certainly a nation like Ghana, which is still heavily dependent on cocoa exports, would benefit significantly from the addition of coffee to its export mix. As Table 2.12 indicates, the

Table 2.11

Correlation of Prices for Various Key Commodities, 1974–1996

	Coffee	Tin	Sugar	Petro.	Cocoa	Bauxite	Rubber
Coffee	1.0000						
Tin	.2715	1.0000					
Sugar	.1436	.0020	1.0000				
Petro.	.0174	.5132	.0054	1.0000			
Cocoa	.6800	.4152	.0982	.0082	1.0000		
Bauxite	.0120	.0002	.0501	.0164	.0040	1.0000	
Rubber	.1051	.0927	.0080	.1816	.0058	.4360	1.000

Note: The export combinations assume equal shares for the two products.

Table 2.12

Coefficient of Variation of Prices for Various Key Commodities, 1974–1996

Products (single or combined)	Variation
Coffee	0.331
Tin	0.386
Sugar	0.459
Petroleum	0.379
Cocoa	0.425
Bauxite	0.286
Rubber	0.228
Rubber–Coffee	0.276
Rubber–Cocoa	0.299
Tin–Rubber	0.352
Sugar–Cocoa	0.352
Sugar–Coffee	0.260
Sugar–Rubber	0.261
Coffee–Cocoa	0.408

coefficient of variation of export prices would fall from 0.425 to 0.408, resulting in greater predictability of export revenues. Facing the most volatile prices of all, sugar producers would benefit from diversification into any of the other goods. With all of the initiatives taken to stabilize the revenues of commodity exporters, it is curious that so little has been done to assist developing nations in reorienting their export mix. This expansion of trade bases would have the added benefit of reducing the production of the perennially overproduced export crops of cocoa, coffee, and sugar.

THE BIRTH OF THE UNCTAD: HOW THE
MOVEMENT TOWARD CARTELS BEGAN

The United Nations Conference on Trade and Development (UNCTAD) became a permanent agency of the United Nations in 1964. At its first formal meeting in Geneva, UNCTAD's agenda was dominated by the trade concerns of a bloc of developing nations known as the Group of 77 (G-77). In the absence of other feasible proposals for reducing the deterioration in trade experienced by commodity exporters, UNCTAD ultimately passed a resolution supporting the formation of cartels.

Despite the support for collusive agreements expressed in the 1964 conference, no cartel accords were signed between the time of the first meeting and the convening of the second round of UNCTAD in New Delhi in 1968. Resolution 16 (II), which was passed unanimously in New Delhi, called for ongoing negotiations regarding the trade of key commodities. The support for the cartel process was strengthened further by Resolution 54 (III) in 1972, which called upon the World Bank and the International Monetary Fund to assist in achieving the goal of price stability. At this point, the cooperation between the developed and developing nations within UNCTAD collapsed, for the United States refused to accept the resolution and most of the other industrialized nations in the organization simply abstained (see McNicol 1978, p. 7).

The approval of Resolution 54 (III) was followed by the passage of the Integrated Program for Commodities (IPC), which was formulated at the UN General Assembly's Special Session on Raw Materials and Development in May 1976. Initially, the IPC pressed for accords for ten key commodity exports: cocoa, coffee, copper, cotton, jute, rubber, sisal, sugar, tea, and tin. Agreements were to come later for eight additional products, including bananas, iron ore, meat, and vegetable oils. The fundamental flaws of the IPC plan soon became apparent. The industrialized nations began to oppose some of the sweeping resolutions passed by UNCTAD and voiced their opposition to the idea of cartelizing most of international commodity trade. It is difficult to imagine how the international markets for copper, cotton, iron ore, meat, sugar, and vegetable oils could be cartelized without the full support of the industrialized countries that also produced these commodities (notably, the United States).

Another flaw of the IPC's plan was its failure to fully endorse buffer stocks as the appropriate means for cartels to regulate prices. As argued by John Maynard Keynes in 1942, buffer stocks are the desired mechanism for eliminating price fluctuations because they do not fundamentally alter prices. This is not necessarily true of alternative commodity arrangements that rely on export controls or quotas. As will be demonstrated in chapter 3, the IPC's promotion of cartelization without buffer stocks doomed the newfound collusive agreements from the start.

UNCTAD's support for the cartel concept was deemed radical at the time. The push toward cartelization was but one initiative of the so-called New Economic Order, the organization's broadly based philosophy of altering the economic relationship between developed and developing nations. This alteration was to be accomplished by establishing a code of "fair" trade by which the relative prices between commodities and manufactured goods were to be manipulated in order to favor the former. Resolution 93, which won majority approval in 1976, expressed UNCTAD's ambitious—if unrealistic—vision of a reformed world economy (see the appendix for text). In order to improve the terms of trade for commodity exporters, the resolution called for the implementation of ten trade measures, most of which clearly worked against free international markets (see Resolution 93, II [2] a-j). In its Proposition II (2) c, the resolution mandated that movements in the prices of imported manufactured goods be taken into account when establishing commodity export prices. Section II (2) d not only proposed the usual supply management measures necessary for the maintenance of any cartel agreement, but also called for the industrialized nations to agree to purchase commitments. Under Section II (2) f, developing nations were encouraged to target export earnings "around a growing trend," a clause that likely pushed cartel members to seek higher, rather than stable, prices.

In the remainder of Resolution 93, UNCTAD promoted the industrialization of commodity-producing nations in the developing world. Section 93 (II) f called for ambitious projects to expand the infrastructure of these countries so that they might assume a greater role in the processing and transport of their products. This section of the resolution also proposed the development of manufacturing sectors to complement the commodity-producing segments of these nations. Section 93 (II) g called for coordinating the output of competing natural and synthetic goods (for example, natural versus synthetic rubber), an initiative that was once more pitted the interests of nonindustrialized nations against those of the developed world. In the end, the United States was so opposed to what it considered to be favoritism toward the developing nations that it refused to accept the resolution.

The timetable for the implementation of UNCTAD's Resolution 93 was unrealistically short. Negotiations on programs for stabilizing the prices of individual commodities were to be concluded by February 1978, that is, less than two years after the issuance of the resolution, and by the end of that year, all aspects of the cartel agreements were to be in effect. To be included in these negotiations were discussions on finances, modes of operation, and management structures for each commodity agreement. Without the active support of the industrialized nations, however, the financial and operational details of Resolution 93 were never worked out and therefore never implemented.

The powerful rhetoric of Resolution 93 obscured the fact that the process of cartelization had already begun in several commodity markets without the intervention of UNCTAD. Moreover, the resolution was drafted during a period when commodity prices were already on the rise and interest in cartels was beginning to ebb. The first International Coffee Agreements, for example, which were signed beginning in 1962, had successfully firmed prices during the 1960s, but when generalized commodity inflation caused coffee prices to surge in the 1970s, exporters lost interest in cartelization. Similarly, the first International Cocoa Agreement was forged in 1972, but by the time a successor accord was signed in 1976, inflation had driven the price of cocoa so high that the new target prices became unnecessary and were never enforced. In this light, it becomes apparent that Resolution 93 constituted a formal statement of a process already under way, and that the G-77's concept of a New Economic Order was not as revolutionary as it may have appeared at the time.

Resolution 93 represented the apex of UNCTAD's influence on international economic policy, and the organization as it exists today is far less ambitious in its agenda. Part of the difficulty for current proponents of "radical" trade reform is that the philosophical differences between the developed and developing nations have narrowed considerably in the last two decades, with the latter adopting many free market practices and benefiting from increased trade. In addition, the diversification of the trade structure of many of the nations that were formerly regarded as single-commodity exporters has made cartels considerably less attractive. Consequently, if the terms of trade are to be significantly altered, then negotiations cannot be drawn along lines that pit industrialized nations against the developing world.

CONCLUSION

The figures presented here demonstrate the extent to which many developing nations relied on commodity exports during the 1970s. The economic health of nations such as Colombia and the Ivory Coast, for example, responded to every movement in the international coffee market, while the growth and development of Saudi Arabia and Venezuela were tied to petroleum prices. Clearly, the very high correlations between real GDP and commodity prices encouraged cartelization. UNCTAD's sweeping proposals for the fundamental revision of world trade, expressed most clearly in Resolution 93, promoted the interests of the developing world so heavy-handedly that the noncooperation of the industrialized nations was inevitable.

By the mid-1980s, the cartel period was largely drawing to a close, as most collusive agreements had either collapsed or ceased to have any real control over commodity prices. By this point, many developing nations had eliminated their dependence on single-commodity exporting, and, as their economies strengthened, the incentive to renew cartel arrangements waned. Nations that had failed to diversify their exports—particularly the petroleum producers of the Middle East—remained committed to the cartel process, yet their unwillingness to make the necessary financial sacrifices undermined their efforts to firm prices.

The ultimate failure of cartels can be traced to a number of factors, including the inherent characteristics of the commodity, the dispersion of production across too many nations, the existence of ready substitutes, and the ease of entry of new producers in response to higher prices. Chapter 3 will detail the history of the seven most important cartelized markets and explore the reasons for the ultimate failure of each. The resulting conclusions will indicate how commodity markets can best be stabilized and insulated against renewed volatility.

NOTES

1. The figures for Saudi Arabia are presented only with a significant delay. As a result, the analysis cannot be carried beyond 1995.

2. Although it is somewhat arbitrary, a drop of approximately 20 percentage points in the export share of each nation's key product was used as an indicator of when diversification had been achieved.

APPENDIX

Resolution 93 (IV) of UNCTAD (presented here in its original form)
Fourth Session
Nairobi, 5 May 1976
Agenda Item 8
Resolution Adopted by the Conference
93 (IV). *Integrated Programme for Commodities*
United Nations Conference on Trade and Development

Recalling the Declaration and the Programme of Action on the Establishment of a New International Economic Order as well as the Charter of Economic Rights and the Duty of States, which lay down the foundations for the new International Economic Order, General Assembly Resolution 623 (VII) of 21 December 1952 and the Conference recommendation A.II.1,

Recalling, in particular, section I, paragraph 3 (a) (iv), of the Programme of Action on the Establishment of a New International Economic Order, relating to the preparation of an over-all integrated programme for "a comprehensive range of commodities of export interest to developing nations,"

Recalling also section I, paragraph 3, of General Assembly resolution 3362 (S-VII) of 16 September 1975, which states, *inter alia*, that "an important aim of the fourth session of the United Nations Conference on Trade and Development, in addition to work in progress elsewhere, should be to reach decisions on the improvement of market structures in the field of raw materials and commodities of export interest to developing countries, including decisions with respect to an integrated programme and the applicability of elements thereof,"

Taking note of the work undertaken on commodities in preparation for the fourth session of the conference, in particular the proposals submitted by the Secretary-General of UNCTAD for an integrated programme for commodities,

Reaffirming the important role of UNCTAD in the field of commodities,

Bearing in mind resolution 16 (VIII) of the Committee on Commodities concerning decisions by the Conference at its fourth session with respect to an integrated programme for commodities, on, *inter alia*:

(a) objectives;
(b) commodities to be covered;

(c) international measures;

(d) follow-up procedures and time-table for the implementation of agreed measures,

Affirming the importance to both producers and consumers, notably developing countries, of commodity exports for foreign exchange earnings and of commodity imports for welfare and economic development,

Recognizing the need to conduct international trade on the basis of mutual advantage and equitable benefits, taking into account the interests of all states, particularly those of the developing countries,

Recognizing also the need for improved forms of international cooperation in the field of commodities which should promote economic and social development, particularly of the developing countries,

Recognizing further the urgent need for substantial progress in stimulating food production in developing countries and the important bearing of international commodity policies on this aim,

Recalling the proposal in the Manila Declaration and Programme of Action for the establishment of a common fund for the financing of international commodity stocks, coordinated national stocks or other necessary measures within the framework of commodity agreements,

Bearing in mind the view that there might be financial savings in operating a central facility for the purpose of financing buffer stocks,

Taking note of the readiness of a number of countries, expressed prior to and at the fourth session of the Conference, to participate in and financially support a common fund,

Noting that there are differences of views as to the objectives and modalities of a common fund,

Convinced of the need for an overall approach and an integrated programme for commodities which is a programme of global action to improve market structures in international trade in commodities of interest to developing countries, and which is consistent with the interests of all countries, particularly those of the developing countries, and assures a comprehensive view of the various elements involved while respecting the characteristics of individual commodities,

Decides to adopt the following Integrated Programme for Commodities:

I. OBJECTIVES

With a view to improving the terms of trade of developing countries and in order to eliminate the economic imbalance between developed and developing nations, concerted efforts should be made in favor of the developing countries towards expanding and diversifying their trade, improving and diversifying their productive capacity, improving their productivity and increasing their export earnings, with a view to counteracting the adverse effects of inflation, thereby sustaining real incomes. Accordingly the following objectives are agreed:

1. To achieve stable conditions in commodity trade, including avoidance of excess price fluctuations, at levels that would:

> (a) Be remunerative and just to producers and equitable to consumers;
> (b) Take into account world inflation and changes in the world economic and monetary situations;
> (c) Promote equilibrium between supply and demand within expanding world commodity trade.

2. To improve and sustain the real income of individual developing countries through increased export earnings, and to protect them from fluctuations in export earnings, especially from commodities.

3. To seek to improve market access and reliability of supply for primary products and the processed products thereof, bearing in mind the needs and interests of developing countries.

4. To diversify production in developing countries, including food production, and to expand processing of primary products in developing countries with a view to promoting their industrialization and increasing their export earnings.

5. To improve the competitiveness of, and to encourage research and development on the problems of, natural products competing with synthetics and substitutes, and to consider the harmonization, where appropriate, of the production of synthetics and substitutes in developed countries with the supply of natural products produced in developing countries.

6. To improve market structures in the field of raw materials and commodities of export interest to developing countries.

7. To improve marketing, distribution, and transport system for commodity exports of developing countries, including an increase in their participation in these activities and their earnings from them.

II. COMMODITY COVERAGE

The commodity coverage of the integrate programme should take into account the interests of developing countries in bananas, bauxite, cocoa, coffee, copper, cotton and cotton yarns, hard fibres and products, iron ore, jute and products, manganese, meat, phosphates, rubber, sugar, tea, tropical timber, tin, and vegetable oils, including olive oil and oilseeds, among others, it being understood that other products could be included, in accordance with the procedure set out in section IV below.

III. INTERNATIONAL MEASURES OF THE PROGRAMME

1. It is agreed that steps will be taken, as described in section IV, paragraphs 1 to 3, below, towards the negotiation of a common fund.

2. It is also agreed to take the following measures, to be applied singly or in combination, including action in the context of international commodity agreements between producers and consumers, in the light of the characteristics and problems of each commodity and the special needs of developing countries:

> (a) Setting up of international commodity stocking arrangements;
> (b) Harmonization of stocking policies and the setting up of coordinated national stocks;
> (c) Establishment of pricing arrangements, in particular negotiated price ranges, which would be periodically reviewed and appropriately revised, taking into account, *inter alia*, movements in prices of imported manufactured goods, exchange rates, production costs and world inflation, and the levels of production and consumption;
> (d) Internationally agreed supply management measures, including export quotas and production policies and, where appropriate, multilateral long-term supply and purchase commitments;
> (e) Improvement of procedures for information and consultation on market conditions;
> (f) Improvement and enlargement of compensatory financing facilities for the stabilization, around a growing trend, of export earnings or developing countries;

(g) Improvement of market access for the primary and processed products of developing countries through multilateral trade measures in the multilateral trade negotiations, improvement of schemes of generalized preferences and their extension beyond the period originally envisioned, and trade promotion measures;

(h) International measures to improve the infrastructure and industrial capacity of developing countries, extending from the production of primary commodities to their processing, transport and marketing, as well as to the production of finished manufactured goods, their transport, distribution and exchange, including the establishment of financial, exchange and other institutions for the remunerative management of trade transactions;

(i) Measures to encourage research and development on the problems of natural products competing with synthetics and consideration of the harmonization where appropriate, of the production of synthetics and substitutes in developed countries with the supply of products produced in developing nations;

(j) Consideration of special measures for commodities whose problems cannot be adequately solved by stocking and which experience a persistent price decline.

3. The interests of developing countries, particularly the least developed and the most seriously affected among them, and those lacking in natural resources, adversely affected by measures under the Integrated Programme, should be protected by means of appropriate differential and remedial measures within the Programme.

4. Special measures, including exemption from financial contributions, should be taken to accommodate the needs of the least developed countries in the Integrated Programme for commodities.

5. Efforts on specific measures for reaching arrangements on products, groups of products, or sectors which, for various reasons, are not incorporated in the first stage of application of the Integrated Programme should be continued.

6. The application of any of the measures which may concern existing international arrangements on commodities covered by the Integrated Programme would be decided by governments within the commodity organizations concerned.

IV. PROCEDURES AND TIMETABLE

1. The Secretary-General of UNCTAD is requested to convene a negotiating conference open to all members of UNCTAD on a common fund no later than March 1977.

2. The Secretary-General of UNCTAD is further requested to convene preparatory meetings prior to the conference referred to in paragraph 1 above concerning, *inter alia*:

(a) Elaboration of objectives;
(b) The financing needs of the common fund and its structure;
(c) Sources of finance;
(d) Mode of operation;
(e) Decision-making and fund management.

3. Member countries are invited to transmit to the Secretary-General of UNCTAD, prior to 30 September 1976, any proposals they may have concerning the above and related issues.

4. The Secretary-General of UNCTAD is further requested to convene, in consultation with international organizations concerned, preparatory meetings for international organizations on individual products, in the period beginning 1 September 1976. These meetings should complete their work as soon as possible, but not later than February 1978. The task of the preparatory meeting shall be to:

(a) Propose appropriate measures and techniques required to achieve the objectives of the Integrated Programme;
(b) Determine financial requirements resulting from the measures and techniques proposed;
(c) Recommend follow-up action required through the negotiation of commodity agreements, or other measures;
(d) Prepare draft proposals of such agreements for the consideration of governments and for use in commodity negotiating conferences.

5. The Secretary-General of UNCTAD is further requested to convene, as and when required, commodity negotiating conferences as soon as possible after the completion of each preparatory meeting held pursuant to paragraph 4 above. These negotiations should be concluded by the end of 1978.

6. The Secretary-General of UNCTAD is requested to undertake the necessary arrangements for the servicing of the preparatory meetings and the subsequent commodity negotiating conferences, in cooperation with the secretariats of the specialized commodity bodies and other organizations concerned.

7. It is agreed that international negotiations or renegotiations on individual commodities covered by existing agreements shall be in accordance with appropriate established procedures for the purpose of concluding international arrangements.

8. The Trade and Development Board is instructed to establish an *ad hoc* intergovernmental committee to coordinate the preparatory work and the negotiations, to deal with major policy issues that may arise, including commodity coverage, and to coordinate the implementation of the measures under the Integrated Programme.

145th Plenary Session
30 May 1976

REFERENCES

Chu, K., and Morrison, T. 1986. "World Non-Oil Primary Commodity Markets." *Staff Papers—International Monetary Fund* 33: 139–184.

Commodity Research Bureau. Various dates. *The Commodity Yearbook.* New York: John Wiley and Sons.

Diakosavvas, D., and Scandizzo, P. 1991. "Trends in the Terms of Trade of Primary Commodities, 1900–1982: The Controversy and Its Origins." *Economic Development and Cultural Change* 38: 231–262.

Grilli, E., and Yang, M. 1988. "Primary Commodity Prices, Manufactured Goods Prices, and the Terms of Trade of Developing Countries: What the Long Run Shows." *World Bank Economic Review* 2, no. 1: 1–46.

Hwa, E. 1979. "Price Determination in Several International Primary Commodity Markets: A Structural Analysis." *Staff Papers—International Monetary Fund* 26: 157–188.

International Monetary Fund. 1988. *International Financial Statistics.* Washington, DC.

Madeley, J. 1993. *Trade and the Poor: The Impact of International Trade on Developing Countries.* New York: St. Martin's Press.

McNicol, D. 1978. *Commodity Agreements and Price Stabilization.* Lexington, MA: D.C. Heath.

3

The History and Evaluation of Significant Commodity Cartels

The phenomenon of collusive international agreements became widespread in the 1930s. At that time, attempts to control production and prices were still mainly the prerogative of multinational firms operating in the developing world. The "modern era" of cartels began in the 1960s, when the governments of developing nations began to participate in commodity agreements. Although this participation significantly altered the institutional structure of cartels, the underlying goals of cartelization remained as they had always been: to increase and stabilize commodity prices.

The following analysis focuses on the role played by commodity cartels active primarily in the developing world. It is through the process of cartelization that exporting nations can attempt to manipulate the world supply and prices of key commodities. The agreements that involve corporations exclusively (notably, the DeBeers diamond empire) will not be discussed until chapter 5. Many of the nations involved in collusive arrangements are single-commodity exporters whose economic health is dependent on a single product. Ideally, commodity agreements offer a means of stabilizing prices and eliminating destructive competition between developing nations.

THE PRIMARY COMMODITY CARTELS OF THE POSTWAR PERIOD

The commodities chosen for examination—coffee, bauxite, cocoa, petroleum, sugar, rubber, and tin—are those for which modern cartel agreements were successfully implemented between 1953 and 1980. Each of

these cartels managed, to varying degrees, to secure meaningful participation by the key exporting countries and, sometimes, importing countries. In all but one instance (the bauxite cartel), mechanisms were put
in place to eliminate excess production and stabilize prices. In contrast
to these examples, other international collusive agreements, such as the
banana cartel, unraveled before the institutional structures and market
controls that characterize cartelization could be realized.

The International Coffee Organization

The International Coffee Organization (ICO) was founded in 1962 for
the purpose of regulating coffee supplies and prices. With the International Coffee Agreement (ICA) of that year, the cartel specified a price
range enforceable through export quotas. Two major producers, Brazil
and Colombia, initiated the agreement in the hope of retaining their re-
spective market shares. Interestingly, the ICA was a contract between
both producing and consuming nations whose goal was to reduce prices
and minimize supply fluctuations. The United States signed the agreement in the hopes of eliminating the volatility of prices that had long
plagued the coffee market. When it became apparent that the target prices
established by the cartel were too high, member nations (particularly
Brazil) were forced to significantly curtail their production. Despite this
gross overvaluation, the agreement was renewed in 1968. The coffee
market then experienced a period of chronic oversupply (and declining
prices) until a frost in the early 1970s devastated the coffee bean crop in
Brazil and restored market equilibrium. The resulting higher prices
caused coffee exporters to lose interest in price controls. Moreover, an
attempt to forge a successor agreement in 1976 stalled because consuming nations balked at the price demands of producing countries. It was
only in 1980 that the exporting nations returned to direct negotiations
with the major importers and the provisions of the 1976 agreement were
finally enforced. This pact necessitated the removal of a substantial quantity of coffee from the market so that prices would firm.

   A more formalized cartel arrangement was put in place with the renewal of the ICA in 1983 (binding until 1986). Under this accord, all
exporting countries agreed to sales quotas to be enforced at the borders
of the importing nations. Unfortunately for the signatories of this ICA,
the excess production resulting from the imposition of export limits was
"dumped" on nonmember nations, thereby weakening prices. Conse-

quently, although the system appeared to be functioning, the cartel price was, in reality, too high. With the expiration of the fourth ICA in October 1989 and the inability to negotiate a successor agreement, coffee was once again traded in an essentially free market.

The overall effectiveness of the cartel can be determined by examining the trends in coffee prices during the tenure of the various ICAs. In 1962, coffee prices stood at $42 per 60-kilogram (132.3-pound) bag (CRB, *Commodity Yearbook*). Between 1962 and 1968, when the second ICA was signed, the price rose to $44 per bag. Subsequently, there was little cooperation on prices and output between producing and consuming nations. Although prices rose rapidly from 1974 onward, increasing by over 15 percent per year until 1980 (Table 3.1), much of the increase owed to the general acceleration of inflation during the 1970s. Subsequently, coffee prices plummeted by over one-third between 1980 and 1981. Thus the cartel's ability to influence prices appears to have been very short-lived.

Despite the inability of the ICAs to maintain coffee prices above their pre-cartel levels, evidence tends to support their effectiveness in reducing price variability. As shown in Table 3.2, the coefficient of variation of coffee prices was lowest from 1976 to 1979 and from 1980 to 1986, that is, during the periods when the cartel was functioning. The greatest price variability took place between 1989 and 1996, after the cartel had dissolved. Thus, although the cartel was largely ineffective in firming the price of coffee, it appears to have achieved at least some improvement in price stability.

Like most cartel agreements, the ICO managed to affect coffee production and prices only sporadically. In contrast to most arrangements, the ICO enlisted both producing and consuming nations in its attempt to stabilize prices, a tactic that failed when it became clear that exporters were actively selling to nonmember countries at below cartel prices. The cartel's demise is attributable to the characteristics of the market itself, for coffee fulfills only three of the five requirements of successful collusive agreements.

First among the requisites of effective cartelization present in the coffee market is the product's nonsubstitutability. During the rapid prices increases of the mid-1970s, for example, attempts to promote coffee substitutes such as chicory in the United States met, understandably, with extreme consumer resistance. The second factor supporting cartelization of the coffee market is the significant barriers to entry into the

Table 3.1

Coffee Production and Prices, 1974–1997 (in millions of 60-kg. bags and in dollars per 60-kg. bag of Colombian beans)

Year	Total Production	New York Price
1974	62.5	102.8
1975	81.7	107.7
1976[a]	73.5	206.8
1977	60.9	318.9
1978	70.9	244.5
1979	78.9	242.1
1980[a]	81.9	254.0
1981	86.3	169.1
1982	98.1	184.4
1983[a]	81.9	173.8
1984	88.8	190.4
1985	90.4	192.1
1986[a]	95.8	256.8
1987	79.4	148.2
1988	103.2	178.3
1989	94.2	141.2
1990	97.0	117.7
1991	100.2	112.2
1992	103.7	84.0
1993	92.9	95.0
1994	93.3	174.2
1995	98.2	214.3
1996	89.9	173.5
1997	100.9	—

Source: Production figures are taken from CRB, *Commodity Yearbook*; prices are derived from IMF, *International Financial Statistics*.
[a]Years in which an ICA was signed or reinstituted.

market, for proper cultivation requires a tropical climate. In addition, the protracted life cycle of coffee trees prevents entry in the near term. Finally, unlike some other critical export crops, coffee can be readily stored across a growing season, enabling cartel members to temporarily remove excess production from the market to support prices.

The two criteria for successful cartelization not met by the coffee market are concentration of production and product homogeneity. The four-country concentration ratio stood at 46.2 percent in 1974 and rose only slightly to 51.9 percent in 1997, percentages below those of an oligopolistic market. (See Tables 3A-1 and 3A-2 for the concentration ratios of key commodity markets.) In 1997, there were fourteen exporting nations with harvests totaling 1 million or more 60-kilogram bags. Given

Table 3.2

Variation in Coffee Prices, 1974–1996

Years	ICA Functioning?	Coefficient of Variation
1976–79	Nominally	0.161
1980–86	Yes	0.168
1976–86	Yes/Nominally	0.198
1989–96	No	0.303

the difficulty of enforcing a quota system among this many producers, it is not surprising that secondary shipments to nations outside the ICO precipitated a breakdown of cooperation among the exporting and importing members. The other major difficulty facing the cartel is the distinction between the various qualities of coffee beans. While the policies of the ICO effectively eliminated any surplus production of higher-quality arabica beans, they stimulated production of lower grade robusto coffees, resulting in a total surplus that caused a permanent disequilibrium.

Were the various ICAs successful in raising the export earnings and welfare of the producing nations? Considering this question for the years from 1982 to 1983, a period during which the ICO's quota system was fully functioning, Herrmann et al. (1993, 136–142) found a significant rise in prices, export revenues, and welfare for the producing nations, and a commensurate reduction in welfare for the importing nations. Although this result tends to support the potential of commodity agreements to increase welfare, it must be recognized that the ICAs were inherently unstable and seldom fully in force. Indeed, the authors noted that one of the ICA's stated goals, increasing world coffee consumption to ensure future demand, was not met, for price increases suppressed demand and reduced the cartel's power in the long run.

The International Bauxite Association and Its Predecessors

Although the International Bauxite Association was founded only in 1974, the market for the metal ore has been subject to some form of cartelization as far back as the 1890s. Prior to that time, the three major producers of aluminum—Alcoa, AIAG of Switzerland, and Froges of France—competed to some degree in the world market. In 1896, Alcoa and AIAG agreed not to export to each other's markets. In 1901, the agreement was expanded to include Froges, Pechiney (another French firm), and British

Aluminium. With this accord, all home markets were effectively closed to competition. In addition, a world price of aluminum was established and each firm was assigned a share of total world demand. Nonetheless, in spite of subsequent agreements made in the years between 1906 and 1911, the bauxite cartel was weakened as new companies entered the market. A further blow was dealt when the Justice Department pressured Alcoa to abandon its participation in any further cartel agreements with its European rivals. The worldwide aluminum industry then entered an extended period of competition that continued into the 1920s.

In 1923, the European aluminum firms informally agreed to limit their exports to the United States. Alcoa responded in kind and prices immediately began to firm. By 1924, prices had risen over 42 percent in the U.S. market and approximately 25 percent in the European market (Holloway 1988, 25). Then, in 1926, a much more strident agreement was created, one that not only established quotas and uniform prices, but also imposed penalties for overproduction. Faced with growing pressure from the Justice Department, Alcoa participated through its Canadian subsidiary, Alcan. In the years following the 1926 agreement, the cartel adopted a number of new provisions that further divided the world aluminum market into proprietary shares. It was only years later, in 1950, that the Justice Department finally forced Alcoa to fully abide by antitrust laws, which resulted in the company's divesting itself of Alcan. (For additional details on the cartelization of the aluminum industry prior to 1950, see Stocking and Watkins 1991.)

A new page in the history of aluminum production was turned in March 1974 with the formation of the International Bauxite Association (IBA). Founded by the prime minister of Jamaica, Michael Manley, and the prime minister of Guyana, Forbes Burnham, the IBA's other member countries were Australia, Guinea, Sierra Leone, Suriname, and Yugoslavia. These nations collectively sought to increase their profits on the exportation of bauxite at the expense of the multinational firms that were extracting the mineral within their borders. Jamaica took the lead by imposing a higher levy on producers, a move that was matched by the cartel's other members. The profitability of bauxite mining among the host countries soon increased significantly.

The peculiar characteristic of the bauxite market that makes it unique among cartels is the fact that there are virtually no integrated aluminum smelting facilities within the bauxite-producing countries of the IBA. Cartel members impose a tax on the raw ore extracted by multinational firms. Thus the IBA's impact on pricing occurs through its tax rather than through the manipulation of world aluminum prices. The integrated aluminum producers acquiesced to the bauxite tax because it represented only a small fraction of the total cost of producing aluminum. Although the price of processed aluminum has risen dramatically since 1974 (Table 3.3), this is mostly the result of rising energy prices. The average levy per metric ton of raw ore, which stood at between five and fifteen dollars in 1974, did not increase again significantly until 1981 (Table 3.4). The most dramatic increases in the per-ton tax occurred in the 1990s, a period characterized by falling aluminum prices. Thus, unlike the other cartels examined here, no connection exists between the increased power of the cartel, the rise in the rate of taxation, and increased prices. It is the nature of the bauxite cartel itself that ensured its success.

The bauxite market was, in fact, well suited to the formation of a cartel, for it conforms to all requirements for collusive agreements. The four-country concentration ratio, which stood at only 54.6 percent in 1974, rose dramatically to 70.3 percent by 1996, a figure well above the level necessary for successful cartelization. Although a total of six "fringe" producers also contributed to the market, their individual shares of total world production were small. A number of substitutes exist for aluminum, but none with the metal's unique properties of malleability combined with low weight. Both the aluminum ore and the finished metal are easily stored if excess supply must be withdrawn from the market. Finally, the recent history of aluminum production has been one of exiting producers (premier among these being the United States), a trend that has reduced competition and kept prices stable.

The defining characteristics of the bauxite market were more relevant for the period preceding 1950 than for subsequent years. The levy system in place since the early 1970s essentially precludes the "producing" countries from utilizing their market power, since all processing and marketing is conducted by the multinational corporations. Nations with significant bauxite deposits benefit from the ability of the major international aluminum firms to pass the prices through to end-users without significantly affecting demand.

The International Cocoa Agreements

In 1963, negotiations began on the establishment of an international cocoa producers organization. These initial talks failed to bring about

Table 3.3

Aluminum Production and Prices, 1974–1996 (in thousands of metric tons and in dollars per metric ton)

Year	Total production	London price
1974	78,362	763.2
1975	73,610	866.6
1976	77,417	888.1
1977	81,931	1,141.4
1978	80,975	1,322.2
1979	85,522	1,599.4
1980	89,215	1,771.2
1981	85,522	1,260.2
1982	77,793	989.6
1983	76,016	1,435.5
1984	92,502	1,248.9
1985	89,747	1,038.6
1986	92,534	1,147.3
1987	96,517	1,561.8
1988	103,105	2,541.2
1989	103,722	1,946.6
1990	113,000	1,636.1
1991	111,000	1,301.3
1992	105,000	1,253.6
1993	109,000	1,137.6
1994	107,000	1,472.5
1995	109,000	1,801.4
1996	—	1,503.7

Source: Production figures are taken from CRB, *Commodity Yearbook*; prices are derived from IMF, *International Financial Statistics*.

an agreement. It was not until 1972 that a successful agreement, the International Cocoa Agreement or ICCA, was negotiated under the auspices of UNCTAD. The producing nations established a system of buffer stocks and export quotas to reduce what had been a persistent oversupply of cocoa on the world market. The first ICCA was never enforced, however, as cocoa prices increased significantly on their own in the year subsequent to the agreement.

The price of cocoa continued to rise into the late 1970s, reaching a peak of $4,038 per ton in 1977 (Table 3.5). The second ICCA was concluded in 1976, just prior to the height in prices. With this agreement, a higher price floor was established, but due to the ever-rising value of cocoa, the target never became binding. Prices then began a significant decline that led to the negotiation of the third ICCA in 1981. This agreement set a target range of $1.00 to $1.50 per pound and restricted total

Table 3.4

Range of Levies Imposed on Bauxite Production (in dollars per metric ton)

Year	Levy	Year	Levy
1974	5–15	1985	13–20
1975	5–15	1986	13–17
1976	5–15	1987	13–17
1977	5–15	1988	13–17
1978	5–15	1989	15–20
1979	5–15	1990	15–20
1980	6–16	1991	15–18
1981	8–20	1992	15–18
1982	8–20	1993	15–24
1983	13–20	1994	15–18
1984	13–20		

Source: CRB, *Commodity Yearbook.*

cartel exports to 250,000 tons, but the nonparticipation of the largest producer of cocoa, the Ivory Coast, resulted in a further deterioration of prices. The cartel's attempt to firm up prices by purchasing nearly 100,000 tons of cocoa in the open market worked only temporarily, and prices continued to fall into 1982. The fourth and final ICCA was concluded in 1986, with new price ranges set this time in special drawings rates. The cartel's additional large purchases of cocoa failed to elevate prices to the target levels. The cocoa market saw its lowest price in 1993, when the commodity sold for only $978 per metric ton, nearly 40 percent below its 1974 level.

The cocoa cartel failed to either stabilize or raise prices. The degree of overproduction was simply too great and the cartel was incapable of buying a sufficient quantity of cocoa to counteract the downward pressure on prices. The entry of new producers such as Malaysia in the 1980s not only further weakened prices but also exerted additional outside pressure on ICCA negotiations. Using a simulation model to estimate the effects of the 1981 and 1986 agreements on the cocoa market, Herrmann et al. (1993, 210) found a reduction in demand for cocoa totaling 89,000 tons as well as an increased supply of 30,000 tons for the period from 1981 to 1989. Their analysis also determined that prices had been increased by only 2 to 4 percent in the wake of the last two ICCAs. Given these results, one must conclude that the International Cocoa Agreements were failures.

Oddly enough, given its unimpressive record, the cocoa market con-

Table 3.5

World Cocoa Production and Prices, 1974–1997 (in thousands of metric tons and in dollars per metric ton)

Year	Total Production	New York Price
1974	1,448	1,613.7
1975	1,547	1,245.0
1976	1,510	1,694.4
1977	1,339	4,037.7
1978	1,512	3,377.7
1979	1,502	3,096.1
1980	1,651	2,355.3
1981	1,694	1,925.0
1982	1,737	1,502.4
1983	1,545	1,828.2
1984	1,545	2,317.0
1985	1,967	2,089.3
1986	1,946	2,024.9
1987	2,014	1,847.1
1988	2,214	1,599.0
1989	2,471	1,250.7
1990	2,419	1,079.5
1991	2,526	1,045.9
1992	2,301	989.8
1993	2,416	978.3
1994	2,519	1,230.0
1995	2,398	1,330.1
1996	2,876	1,409.5
1997	2,660	—

Sources: Production figures are taken from CRB, *Commodity Yearbook;* prices are derived from IMF, *International Financial Statistics.*

forms to many of the conditions necessary for cartelization. The four-country concentration ratio stood at 72.1 percent in 1997, a level certainly high enough for successful cooperation. Although artificial flavorings can imitate the taste of cocoa, for most purposes the real item is utilized. Cocoa beans are nonperishable, enabling a working cartel to adjust stocks to prevailing demand. Spar (1994, 261) noted that some differentiation exists among cocoa beans, yet the ICCA negotiations did not appear to be disrupted by this. The primary challenge to profitability for the cartel was permanent overproduction, which was only worsened by the group's deliberate inflation of prices. Despite a 35 percent drop in the world price of cocoa from 1981 to 1989 (Table 3.5), production rose by 46 percent. In addition, the entry of Malaysia into the market in 1986 demonstrated that the barriers to entry in the cocoa market could be overcome. Thus the market continued to be plagued by a growing over-supply, which explains the de facto collapse of the ICCA after 1990.

The Organization of Petroleum Exporting Countries

The Organization of Petroleum Exporting Countries (OPEC) was formed in September 1960 in response to a developing weakness in the price of oil. In addition, OPEC members wanted to increase their share of the profits enjoyed by the multinational firms (primarily from the United States and Great Britain) that extracted and marketed their petroleum resources. The softening of prices resulting from a variety of economic and political factors led to a substantial surplus in the oil markets by the late 1950s. First, voluntary import restrictions imposed by the United States in 1957 were made mandatory in 1959, significantly reducing demand. Second, new producers of petroleum, particularly the USSR, were beginning to influence supply to the detriment of existing export-ers. Finally, in the latter part of the decade, the international oil market was adversely affected by a surplus of tanker traffic, which led to addi-tional competition and falling prices (see Ghanem 1986, 71–74, for ad-ditional details). By 1960, the price received by OPEC members had declined by 15 to 20 percent (depending on the grade of petroleum). At the time, it was projected that petroleum prices would continue to fall into the foreseeable future. Consequently, OPEC sought a return to the prices that had prevailed earlier in the decade.

OPEC membership has generally been confined to countries in the Middle East and North Africa. The original signatories—Iran, Iraq, Kuwait, Saudi Arabia, and Venezuela—were joined by Qatar in 1961, Libya and Indonesia in 1962, and Algeria in 1969. Abu Dhabi became a member in 1967, but was later absorbed into the United Arab Emirates. The ranks of OPEC further expanded in the ensuing years with the entry of Nigeria in 1971, Ecuador in 1973, and Gabon in 1975. Despite its growing membership, OPEC was only gradually able to achieve its goal of manipulating prices by controlling world production of petroleum.

In spite of the regularity of its meetings during the early 1960s, OPEC failed to significantly increase the prevailing price of crude oil. The perennial problem of worldwide overproduction was complicated by the refusal of international oil companies to boost petroleum prices. The situation did not change until September 1, 1969, when the government of Libya was overthrown in a coup by Colonel Muammar Qaddafi, who immediately took a hard line with the multinational oil firms. By September 1970, Occidental Oil had agreed to increase the price of Libyan crude by $0.30 per barrel, and within a few months, all petroleum firms operating in Libya had agreed to the new terms. Recognizing the impossibility of maintaining the new pricing structure with Libya in the absence of similar price increases for oil originating elsewhere, the multinationals increased petroleum prices by $0.20 to $0.25 for Middle Eastern crude. This represented OPEC's first real success in securing higher prices.

The notoriety of OPEC arose from its ability to manipulate the price of petroleum during the period from 1973 to 1980. The cartel's apparent effectiveness in controlling oil markets was somewhat illusory, however, being more the result of international conflict than of its inherent power. In September 1973, Egypt and Syria went to war against Israel in an attempt to regain land lost in previous conflicts. The international oil markets immediately tightened, and in October, OPEC members from the Gulf region increased their crude oil prices. These same producers decided to punish Israel's key ally, the United States, by placing an embargo on all shipments to the States (sales to the Netherlands were also forbidden). In addition, OPEC instituted its first significant tightening of petroleum supplies when it decreed a 5 percent reduction in world oil shipments.

As shown in Table 3.6 and Figure 3.1, the impact of this measure on world oil prices was immediate. While the price of crude had crept up slowly during the early 1970s—to an average price of $3.14 by 1973—the cost per barrel rose nearly 260 percent to $11.22 by 1974. After fourteen relatively frustrating years of attempting to firm prices, the members of OPEC finally saw a significant rise in the value of their oil exports. Due to the inelasticity of demand for petroleum (at least in the short run), OPEC was able to hold to these prices without producing a drop in the imports of the industrialized nations. These increases slowed after 1974, with the price of crude rising to $12.95 per barrel by 1978. The key problem for OPEC during this period was that the substantially higher price of oil stimulated production from non-OPEC producers. Hence it was not declining demand but rather the arrival of new sources of petroleum on the world market that kept OPEC in check from 1974 to 1978.

The next significant expression of OPEC's power, once again, arose more from international conflict than from the inherent ability of the cartel to control the oil market. The sensitivity of petroleum prices to

Table 3.6

Petroleum Production and Prices, 1970–1996 (in thousands of barrels per day and in dollars per barrel)

Year	Daily Production	Average Price
1970	45,731	2.11
1971	48,397	2.57
1972	50,967	2.80
1973	55,808	3.14
1974	56,274	11.22
1975	53,425	10.60
1976	58,066	11.83
1977	59,803	12.84
1978	60,057	12.95
1979	62,535	29.22
1980	59,538	36.68
1981	55,900	35.27
1982	53,458	32.45
1983	52,981	29.66
1984	54,488	28.56
1985	53,981	27.31
1986	56,227	14.23
1987	56,666	18.15
1988	58,737	14.72
1989	59,863	17.84
1990	60,566	22.97
1991	60,207	19.33
1992	60,216	19.03
1993	61,358	16.82
1994	61,358	15.90
1995	62,230	17.16
1996	63,821	20.42

Sources: Production figures are taken from CRB, *Commodity Yearbook*; prices are derived from IMF, *International Financial Statistics*.

small supply reductions was demonstrated after the revolution in Iran in late 1978, when that country's 60 percent reduction in output resulted in the elevation of world oil prices from $12.95 in 1978 to $29.22 per barrel in 1979. OPEC was able to maintain most of this increase for the next six years, with prices only gradually moving down to $27.31 by 1985. Conservation efforts on the part of the industrialized nations and the increased number of non-OPEC producing nations precipitated a 50 percent drop in prices, to just $14.23 per barrel in 1986. It was at this point that many observers began to regard OPEC as a faltering, if not broken, cartel.

Although OPEC exercised some power over petroleum markets be-

Figure 3.1   **Petroleum Prices, 1970–1997**

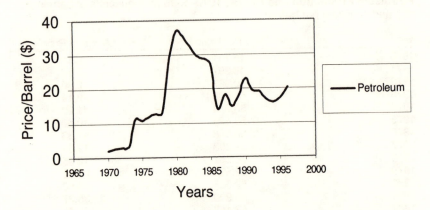

tween 1973 and 1986, and despite the fact that it fulfills some of the necessary conditions for cartelization, such as product homogeneity, the international oil market fails to meet two criteria. First, the barriers to entry that would prevent competition from additional producers are very weak. Second, as noted above, the rapid price increases realized under OPEC's tenure provided a strong incentive for nonmembers to discover new petroleum resources and expand existing ones. Thus oil production in Mexico, which was just over 500,000 barrels per day in 1973, grew to nearly 2.5 million barrels per day by 1986 (CRB, *Commodity Yearbook*). Similarly, China, which was not a major exporter of petroleum in 1973, nearly doubled its production to 2.6 million barrels per day by 1986 (CRB, *Commodity Yearbook*). As new producers entered the market and traditional suppliers expanded their production, OPEC's share of the world oil market began a long decline, falling from over 50 percent of world production in 1973 to just slightly over 45 percent by 1980, and then to less than 30 percent by 1985 (Table 3.7). Not surprisingly, a price collapse occurred in 1986 when Saudi Arabia, in a desperate attempt to induce its cartel partners to negotiate seriously, flooded the market with oil. By this point, OPEC's clout in world oil markets had become negligible.

The second factor that disempowered the cartel during the 1980s was the substitution of alternative energy sources for oil. Although there are no alternatives for some petroleum uses (primarily, of course, the traditional internal combustion engine), as the price of crude increased, de-

Table 3.7

OPEC's Share of Total World Production, 1970–1986 (as a percentage)

Year	%
1970	48.6
1971	52.1
1972	52.7
1973	55.4
1974	54.2
1975	50.9
1976	52.8
1977	52.3
1978	49.7
1979	49.4
1980	45.2
1981	40.4
1982	35.5
1983	32.1
1984	30.4
1985	28.5
1986	32.6

Source: CRB, *Commodity Yearbook.*

mand for substitutes such as coal and natural gas rose. Thus, after the major price increases of 1979 and 1980, world petroleum shipments fell from over 62 million barrels per day in 1979 to under 53 million barrels in 1983, a decline of nearly 15 percent. The volume of shipments did not rebound to their 1979 levels until 1990.

The undoing of OPEC's power was also partly attributable to the tendency of member nations to cheat once the cartel had achieved some degree of monopoly power (see chapter 1 for an analysis of these quota violations). As demand for petroleum declined in the early 1980s, it became increasingly difficult for OPEC members to maintain the cartel's benchmark price. Finally, in January 1982, the prices of some grades of petroleum were cut. This measure, however, did not end the glut of oil in the market. Faced with declining revenues, individual producers began offering various discounts, frequently coupled with extended payment terms. By December 1992, price cuts had become the norm, and the international price of oil began to slide precipitously. Even when demand for petroleum recovered later in the 1990s, OPEC remained an effete cartel, with little power to manipulate world production or prices until very recently.

The International Sugar Controls

The first attempts to regulate sugar production and pricing arose out of the deterioration of the sugar market in the mid-1920s. The price per pound, which had been as high as $0.11 in 1920, had fallen to just under $0.03 in 1925. This drop had resulted in a massive reduction in the revenues of sugar producers, with Cuban suppliers particularly hard-hit. On October 4, 1927, Congress passed legislation that allowed the president to impose production quotas on Cuban producers. The resulting restriction in output led to some temporary firming of sugar prices in the late 1920s. Cuban production fell by over 1.3 million tons, from 5.8 million tons in 1925 to 4.6 million tons in 1928 (Stocking and Watkins 1991, 29). Despite this action by the United States, the world price of sugar began to decline sharply in 1929 and the quota system was abandoned.

The Cuban experience is instructive because it represents a unilateral attempt to manipulate international prices and production. It should have been obvious to both the United States and the sugar-producing firms that the quota system was doomed to fail in the absence of some form of international cooperation. This is because while Cuba was the dominant exporter of sugar in 1927, it was responsible for less than 20 percent of total world production. Thus, while the production quotas had a significant affect on Cuba's output, the impact of these measures on total world production was negligible.

The international initiative to reduce the persistent oversupplies of sugar dates to 1931, when industry representatives from Belgium, Cuba, Czechoslovakia, Germany, Hungary, Java, and Poland signed the Chadbourne Plan, which held its signatories to export limits for the ensuing five years. Notably absent from these negotiations were representatives of American and British sugar producers, a situation that suggested that the Chadbourne Plan would likely experience many of the same problems that had plagued the unilateral Cuban restrictions. Indeed, the plan did nothing to firm prices during its five-year tenure. The price of sugar declined to a low of $0.59 per pound in 1932 and recovered only slightly after that (Stocking and Watkins 1991, 39). Although Cuba and Java adhered to the agreement and faithfully cut production and exports, their efforts were offset by the increased production of countries outside the Chadbourne Plan.

It was futile to try to revive the plan when it expired in 1935. An alternative attempt at cartelization was undertaken in 1937, with producers and consumers now joining to regulate both supply and demand. Unlike the Chadbourne Plan, the cartel of 1937 was an intergovernmental arrangement involving twenty-one countries that controlled 90 percent of world production and consumption (Stocking and Watkins 1991, 43–44). The 1937 agreement established export quotas for the major producers and reserve quotas for nations that intermittently released excess production onto the world market. As noted by Stocking and Watkins, rather than directly addressing the problem of worldwide oversupply, the agreement focused on preventing additional import restrictions by nations like the United States. By restricting exports, the cartel managed to increase sugar prices by approximately 30 percent. This increase, nonetheless, represented an absolute increase of only .30 cents (from 1.03 to 1.34 cents per pound), hardly significant enough to improve economic circumstances in the producing countries.

The failure of the 1937 agreement did not dissuade the sugar-producing nations from further attempts at cartelization. With Cuba in the lead, the first International Sugar Agreement (ISA) was signed in 1953. Like the attempts made in the 1920s to address the oversupply of sugar through the restrictions imposed on a single producer, the 1953 accord relied primarily on Cuba to manage exports. As noted by Spar (1994, 223), with its production level centralized under governmental control, the Cuban sugar industry was well suited to act as the world's manager of supply, for it could raise or lower output to fit market conditions. In addition, while sugar production was widely distributed internationally, the export market was dominated by Cuba through the 1970s. The ISA succeeded in maintaining the target price of sugar through 1955, but a poor European harvest of sugar beets in 1956 resulted in an increase in prices beyond target levels. The second ISA, which was in force from 1959 to 1963, managed to keep prices within range until the final year of the agreement, at which time the U.S. embargo on Cuban exports forced the excess production of the latter onto the world market. Although additional ISAs were signed in 1968 and 1977, they proved to be largely irrelevant in the face of falling production in Cuba and the former Soviet Union, which eventually led to a fivefold increase in the price per pound (Table 3.8). Unfortunately for sugar producers, this resulted in a sizable increase in world output, and prices collapsed in 1985.

As noted by Gilbert (1987), the ISAs were far less successful in managing prices than other collusive agreements of the same period. For one thing, the various ISAs lacked any supply-management system and

Table 3.8

Sugar Production and Prices, 1974–1997 (in thousands of metric tons and in dollars per metric ton)

Year	Total Production	New York Price
1974	80,488	558.4
1975	78,620	642.0
1976	81,888	253.4
1977	86,913	181.3
1978	92,065	169.4
1979	90,170	193.4
1980	84,560	479.4
1981	88,466	372.2
1982	100,555	207.2
1983	101,348	208.1
1984	95,553	201.7
1985	97,546	146.5
1986	98,798	154.7
1987	103,951	149.6
1988	103,786	185.2
1989	105,562	267.1
1990	108,772	350.7
1991	113,484	261.1
1992	116,512	244.6
1993	112,088	255.4
1994	109,787	289.1
1995	115,842	302.5
1996	122,509	290.4
1997	124,989	—

Source: Production figures are taken from CRB, *Commodity Yearbook;* prices are derived from IMF, *International Financial Statistics.*

relied instead on export controls of participating nations. Market conditions produced rapid price increases that created an incentive for new producers to enter the market. By the time the fourth ISA expired in 1983, production had become far more diversified and difficult to control. Thus the sugar cartel's failure was due, at least in part, to an inability to control prices on the upside. Despite the lack of barriers to entry and the diffusion of production among too many producers, the sugar market meets other requirements for successful cartelization. If one is careful to include all sources of sugar (notably cane and beet), then a suitable substitute for sugar does not really exist. The product is nonperishable, at least in the short term, and is considered (at least in the Western diet) to be a necessity. In conclusion, the ISAs might have been more successful if world production had not been so diffuse.

The Natural Rubber Agreements

The market for natural rubber is probably the most complex of the international commodity markets, for its producers must compete with a near perfect substitute: synthetic rubber. This substitutability places a significant constraint on the degree to which the producers of natural rubber can increase or stabilize prices. On the positive side for the members of any potential cartel, natural rubber production is highly concentrated, with only five nations responsible for nearly 90 percent of world output. Consequently, although it is unlikely that a cartel could significantly raise the price of rubber, certain mechanisms for stabilizing prices can be implemented.

As with most commodity markets, cartelization in the rubber industry has an early history during which rubber-producing firms sought a means by which to reduce oversupply. In 1920, the British firms that made up the largest segment of membership in the Rubber Growers' Association cut production by 25 percent. Although purely voluntary, these production restrictions were widely supported by both British and Dutch firms. Unfortunately for the association, however, American rubber producers, which were heavily overstocked, did not endorse the quotas. Rubber prices subsequently fell, bottoming out at less than $0.17 per pound in 1921. The recovery of prices later that year, however, made renegotiating the output quotas impossible. In devising the Stevenson Plan in 1922, British producers acted unilaterally to reduce world production by setting export quotas. Although the dramatic rise in rubber prices in the ensuing years seems to demonstrate the effectiveness of the Stevenson Plan, the recovery in the natural rubber market probably owes more to the accelerating pace of economic expansion in the industrialized nations.

The onset of the Great Depression, coupled with the development in the 1920s of the first synthetic rubbers, resulted in considerable weakness in natural rubber markets. By 1933, the price had fallen to less than $0.04 per pound, down over 95 percent from its high of $0.73 in 1925. In desperation, the governments of the major rubber-producing nations once again sought to establish a workable cartel. In 1934, the International Rubber Agreement (IRA) was concluded, with its signatories— France, India, the Netherlands, Siam, and the United Kingdom—agreeing to quotas enforced through the use of penalties for excess exports.

The IRA succeeded in controlling both supply and prices. A major problem for the cartel was the existence of excessive stocks of raw rubber; in 1934, stockpiled rubber represented nearly nine months of normal demand (Stocking and Watkins 1991, 80). By restricting output to 70 percent of that permitted under the quotas set by this agreement, both the excess supply and stockpiles began to fade, reducing the holdings of rubber to less than a six-month supply by 1936 (Stocking and Watkins 1991, 82). Prices recovered rapidly, so that by 1937, rubber was selling for over $0.19 per pound. Although this represented a major accomplishment for the cartel, rubber prices remained substantially below their 1920 levels. The IRA, which was extended twice, in 1938 and again in 1943, came to an end during World War II, in April 1944.

Interestingly, the major producers of synthetic rubber developed their own collusive schemes to control supply. These measures primarily involved self-imposed restrictions on production in exchange for access to improved technology for the production of synthetics. Although this history is fascinating, it falls outside the concerns of this analysis (for this history, see Stocking and Watkins 1991, 87–117).

The most recent phase of cartelization of the rubber market dates to the signing in October 1980 of the Natural Rubber Agreement (NRA), whose major goal was the elimination of price fluctuations through the creation of a buffer stock of up to 550,000 tons of the commodity. The accord also established critical prices that were to act as a guide for the manager of the buffer stock.[1] The price of rubber fell substantially during the first two years of the accord, prompting additions to the buffer stock in 1982. Similarly, the price dipped close to the "must-buy" range in 1985, leading to further purchases. A very rapid price recovery then occurred, leading to the dispersal of the buffer stocks accumulated in the earlier period. By 1988, the buffer stocks were down to less than 5 percent (approximately 25,000 tons) of their maximum permissible level. Despite a renewal of the agreement in 1987, rubber demand and prices began to fall as world automobile and tire markets softened in advance of the U.S. recession of 1991. Prices bottomed out in 1993, when rubber sold for only $990 per ton, a value below the 1982 level.

The correspondence between the business cycle, automobile and tire production, and the price of natural rubber can be seen in Table 3.9. As illustrated in Figure 3.2, rubber prices followed a path similar to that of other renewable commodities. The recessions of 1974–1975, 1982, and 1991–1992 dampened demand for automobiles in the United States, which led to weakness in natural rubber demand. Similarly, the slow-down in GDP growth in 1986 also resulted in a decline in prices. Thus, although the rubber cartel was able to somewhat dampen price fluctuations, the level of economic activity in the industrial world still predominated. Was the cartel able to reduce the variability of prices after 1980? The standard deviation of prices fell from 314.1 during the period from 1974 to 1980 to 126.9 in the years from 1981 to 1989. Although this reduction in variability was accompanied by a slight decrease in the average price paid for rubber, the cartel's members benefited enormously from the reduced uncertainty of demand. (Additional evaluations of the performance of the IRAs can be found in Herrmann et al. 1993, 165–197; and Burger and Smit 1990.)

Although they achieved only limited success, the Natural Rubber Agreements benefited both consumers and producers by measurably reducing price variability. Several characteristics of the rubber market made it conducive to cartelization. The four-country concentration ratio of the natural rubber market stood at 83.3 percent in 1980, at the time the cartel was formed, and dropped only slightly, to 81.3 percent, in 1994. Both of these ratios are well above the level considered necessary for the successful operation of a cartel. The barriers to entry in natural rubber production are considerable (although not insurmountable). Thus while Brazil was one of the top ten producers in the early 1980s, by the 1990s it had been superseded by a new entrant, Vietnam. While the entry of additional producers is possible, it is likely to have minimal impact on the success of the cartel. Instead of achieving its price targets through production quotas, which are always difficult to enforce in a large cartel, the Natural Rubber Agreement functioned through the use of a buffer stock. Although the rubber market could have been overwhelmed by the entry of numerous new producers, the cartel was able to stabilize prices without the explicit cooperation of all the existing rubber exporters. In addition, rubber can be characterized as a fairly homogeneous product, which eliminated any need for complex pricing schemes.

The most difficult problem for the cartel was the substitutability of synthetic rubber. The production of synthetics had grown from 7.6 million metric tons in 1974 (31.3 percent of world production of all rubber commodities) to over 8.8 million metric tons by 1994 (39.4 percent of world output). Therefore, although the four-country concentration ratio in the natural rubber industry is high, if recalculated as a percentage of total rubber production, it is, in fact, rather low (28.8 percent in 1994).

Table 3.9

Natural Rubber Production and Prices, 1974–1995 (in thousands of metric tons and in dollars per metric ton)

Year	Production	New York Price
1974	3,445	875.6
1975	3,315	657.8
1976	3,575	869.0
1977	3,605	915.2
1978	3,715	1,091.2
1979	3,770	1,432.2
1980	3,850	1,606.0
1981	3,705	1,267.2
1982	3,750	996.6
1983	4,025	1,232.0
1984	4,260	1,091.2
1985	4,400	919.6
1986	4,490	943.8
1987	4,840	1,111.0
1988	5,020	1,278.7
1989	5,150	1,108.8
1990	5,120	1,018.6
1991	5,240	1,005.4
1992	5,460	1,018.9
1993	5,340	990.0
1994	5,720	1,313.4
1995	—	1,810.6

Source: CRB, *Commodity Yearbook.*

The signatories of the Natural Rubber Agreements realized the futility of raising prices under these circumstances, and concentrated instead on maintaining prices. The success of the natural rubber cartel is therefore at least partially attributable to its fairly modest goals.

The International Tin Cartel

The foundations of the International Tin Cartel date to 1931, when representatives of the major producing countries—Bolivia, China, Malaysia (represented by the United Kingdom), the Netherlands, and the United Kingdom—sought to stabilize falling prices by adopting a set of supply restrictions, production carryovers, and price objectives. Even before the four-year implementation period had passed, a second agreement was struck by the signatories in 1933. The third agreement added a new entrant, Siam (Thailand), whose demands forced the existing members to accede to extremely high production quotas. Although the expansion

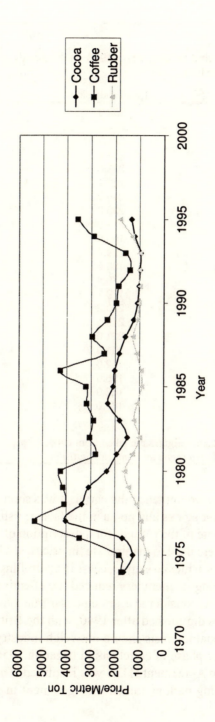

Figure 3.2 Coffee, Cocoa, and Rubber Prices, 1974–1997

Table 3.10

Tin Production and Prices, 1974–1996 (in thousands of metric tons and in dollars per metric ton)

Year	Total Production	London Price
1974	232.9	8,167.1
1975	224.2	6,862.2
1976	225.3	7,569.8
1977	231.4	10,781.8
1978	235.0	12,848.2
1979	241.1	15,415.0
1980	245.9	16,742.7
1981	238.0	14,139.4
1982	219.9	12,802.9
1983	196.9	12,960.4
1984	198.4	12,204.7
1985	188.6	11,514.8
1986	179.4	6,148.6
1987	179.7	6,675.9
1988	200.2	7,036.9
1989	216.5	8,516.6
1990	221.0	6,072.7
1991	201.0	5,584.3
1992	182.0	6,091.8
1993	195.0	5,156.8
1994	182.0	5,448.5
1995	187.0	6,184.4
1996	—	6,145.9

Sources: Production figures are taken from CRB, *Commodity Yearbook*; prices are derived from IMF, *International Financial Statistics*.

of membership strengthened the cartel, it was soon forced to institute a system of buffer stocks and pools in the face of rising production in the nonmember state of the Congo (for a description of how these two market controls were used to manipulate tin prices, see Hillman 1988, 250–253). The cartel achieved some success in controlling prices, but constant infighting among its members reduced the effectiveness of these measures. As tin was considered a strategic wartime mineral, support for the cartel's actions diminished after 1940, with the British arguing forcibly that international interests should outweigh industry profits.

The postwar phase of cartelization began in 1956, when the first International Tin Agreement (ITA) was instituted. The United States and other consuming nations joined the agreement in an attempt to bring about greater price stability. The provisions of the initial ITA were re-newed four times, with each agreement establishing higher target prices. The relative success of the cartel can be seen in the movement of prices during the latter half of the 1970s (Table 3.10). After reaching a low of $6,862.2 per metric ton in 1975, prices rebounded to nearly $17,000 per ton in 1980, an increase of over 144 percent. In 1981, the final year of the fifth ITA, the United States withdrew its support from the cartel and prices declined rapidly during the first half of the 1980s. In 1996, prices had still not returned to their 1974 levels.

Despite their eventual collapse, the ITAs were successful in keeping tin prices close to the target ranges for the period from 1956 to 1981 period (see Gilbert 1987, 609). The high concentration ratio in this mar-ket (nearly 70 percent) made cooperation on production quotas pos-sible. The geographic distribution of tin ore is narrow, preventing the entry of additional producers in response to price increases. The cartel managed the international market through the effective use of an inter-national buffer stock, coupled with export controls. These factors tended to make the ITAs function far better than other commodity agreements. As noted by Gilbert, however (1987, 610), the market's one wild card was the stockpile of strategic reserves of tin held by the United States, which in 1956 were equivalent to six years of domestic consumption. Although the United States made an effort to carefully manage the re-lease of tin from its stockpile, the cartel's control of prices was always dependent on U.S. restraint. In addition, Anderson and Gilbert (1988) noted that the ITAs frequently targeted prices at an unmaintainable level, acting as if establishing a price floor rather than price stability was the goal. This misstep led to market disequilibrium, with the downward price pressure leading to the demise of the International Tin Agreement.

THE INTERNATIONAL COMMODITY CARTELS: AN EVALUATION

Although it would be erroneous to assert that all commodity arrange-ments are destined to fail, the analyses carried out above suggest that cartels accomplish far less than their signatories set out to achieve. In addition, collusive agreements appear to be fairly fragile, even in indus-tries whose market characteristics are most conducive to cartelization. OPEC, the most notorious of the modern cartels, functioned most effec-tively for only thirteen years. In fact, the very features that had made the

Table 3.11

Characteristics of Selected Commodity Markets in 1974

Market	Concentrated	Barriers	Non-substitut-ability	Storability	Homogeneous
Petroleum	Yes	Weak	Strong	High	Yes
Bauxite	Yes	Strong	Moderate	High	Yes
Sugar	No	Weak	Strong	Short-Term	Yes
Coffee	No	Moderate	Strong	Short-Term	No
Rubber	Yes	Moderate	Moderate	High	Yes
Tin	Yes	Strong	Moderate	High	Yes
Cocoa	No	Moderate	Moderate	Short-Term	Yes

formation of OPEC feasible, in particular the low elasticity of demand, led to its downfall in 1986, for increased market power resulted in rapid diversification of petroleum production among nonmember nations.

Characteristics of Commodity Cartels

Table 3.11 summarizes the characteristics of the various markets discussed in the previous section. In only four of the seven markets considered was the four-country concentration ratio high enough to enable the cartel to successfully manage both output and pricing. By the mid-1990s, this number had dropped to three, when the concentration ratio of the petroleum market fell to only 38 percent. As for the barriers to entry, only the bauxite and tin suppliers enjoyed market exclusivity. For the rest, the price increases brought about by cartelization inevitably resulted in the entry of additional producers. The nonsubstitutability criterion was fulfilled by the coffee, petroleum, and sugar industries. For the other four products, however, increased prices led to the introduction of substitutes by the consuming nations, thereby weakening the power of the cartels. Even with the shorter storage limits for cocoa, coffee, and sugar, all seven markets met the criterion of nonperishability. Finally, in six of the seven industries, the product could be considered homogeneous. The exception to this is coffee, for which the absence of homogeneity became a vexing problem. In summary, except for bauxite, the commodity markets under consideration failed to meet one or more of the criteria necessary for successful collusive agreements. These shortcomings explain the instability of commodity cartels and their inability to control production and prices in the long-term.

Despite the eventual demise of most cartels, it could be argued that members of collusive agreements benefit from the temporarily higher prices brought about by the coordination of supply. Yet this assertion is

Table 3.12

Variability in Prices of Cartelized and Noncartelized Commodities, 1974–1991 (coefficient of variation in prices)

Commodity	Price Variability
Cocoa	.428
Petroleum	.391
Sugar	.483
Tin	.386
Copper	.269
Nickel	.402
Rubber	.181
Zinc	.236

difficult to test. For example, it is impossible, ex post, to establish the path that petroleum prices would have taken in the absence of OPEC. Similarly, one cannot readily determine the price that would have prevailed in the coffee market in the absence of the various ICAs. One could, however, compare the experiences of cartelized markets with other commodity trade, in terms of both price trends and price stability. For the former, the long-term path of commodity prices is determined by a variety of factors, many of which are wholly beyond the control of the cartel (namely, changes in demand due to changes in technology or in the cost of other inputs). Conversely, achieving at least some reduction in price variability is a core objective of every cartel.

It is instructive to compare the price variability of three noncartelized commodities—copper, nickel, and zinc—with the price deviations of the cartelized resources already discussed (Table 3.12). The highest degree of price stability (as measured by the coefficient of variation) was achieved in the cartelized rubber market, closely followed by the zinc and copper markets. For the two most volatile markets, sugar and cocoa, cartelization did little to eliminate price fluctuations. From these figures, it would appear that cartels are no better at achieving price stability than unmanaged commodity markets.

Cartels and the Commodity Terms of Trade

The fundamental problem for commodity producers, particularly developing nations, is the decline in the relative price of their exports versus the manufactured goods that they must import. If, for example, the price of cocoa fails to keep pace with the increasing price of industrial products, then cocoa exporters must increase their foreign sales simply to

Table 3.13

Price of Manufactured Goods Exported by the G-5 to Developing Nations, 1974–1982

Year	Index
1974	56.5
1975	62.8
1976	63.7
1977	69.9
1978	80.5
1979	91.2
1980	100.0
1981	100.4
1982	98.9
1983	96.6
1984	94.5
1985	95.3
1986	112.4
1987	123.4
1988	132.4
1989	131.5
1990	138.9
1991	141.8

Source: IMF, *International Financial Statistics.*

Figure 3.3   **Relative Price of Coffee, Cocoa, Sugar, and Rubber, 1974–1991**

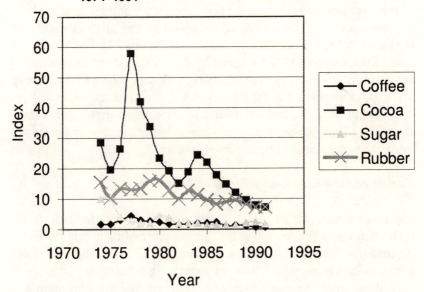

Figure 3.4   **Relative Price of Petroleum and Tin, 1974–1991**

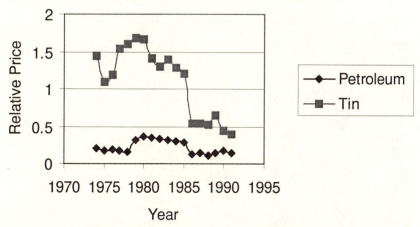

maintain the existing level of import revenues. Exporters, however, cannot raise production without causing a severe and self-defeating decline in the price of the commodity. Consequently, one of the major goals of any cartel is to control oversupply and prevent a decline in the terms of trade facing producers.

How successful have the various cartel arrangements been in maintaining or improving the terms of trade of member nations? Table 3.13 contains the World Bank's price index for manufactured goods exported by G-5 countries to developing nations for the years 1974 through 1991. Over this period, the price of G-5 exports rose by over 5.5 percent per year (this despite some significant weakness in prices between 1981 and 1986). These figures can be used to create a relative price for key commodities exported by the developing nations.

Table 3.14 and Figures 3.3 and 3.4 show the price of various cartelized commodities versus the price of manufactured exports from the industrialized nations. Although there are important differences in the pattern of prices for each commodity, some generalizations can be made. The producers saw their greatest gains during the period from 1975 to 1980. From 1980 onward, however, a general downward trend can be observed in all six commodities. By 1991, cocoa's relative price had fallen approximately 75 percent from its 1974 level, and during the same period, sugar depreciated in value by over 80 percent.

The deterioration in the terms of trade for each of these commodities took place despite the existence of active cartels. The mixed results of cartelization are demonstrated by the ICAs, for the 1980 agreement was

Table 3.14

Relative Price of Commodity Exports, 1974–1991

Year	Coffee	Cocoa	Petroleum	Sugar	Rubber	Tin
1974	1.82	28.6	0.20	9.88	15.5	144.5
1975	1.71	19.8	0.17	10.22	10.5	109.3
1976	3.25	26.6	0.19	3.98	13.6	118.8
1977	4.56	57.8	0.18	2.59	13.1	154.2
1978	3.04	42.0	0.16	2.10	13.6	159.6
1979	2.65	33.9	0.32	2.12	15.7	169.0
1980	2.54	23.6	0.37	4.79	16.1	167.4
1981	1.68	19.2	0.35	3.71	12.6	140.8
1982	1.86	15.2	0.33	2.10	10.1	129.5
1983	1.80	18.9	0.31	2.15	12.8	139.2
1984	2.01	24.5	0.30	2.13	11.5	129.2
1985	2.02	21.9	0.29	1.54	9.6	120.8
1986	2.28	18.0	0.13	1.38	8.4	54.7
1987	1.20	15.0	0.15	1.21	9.0	54.1
1988	1.35	12.1	0.11	1.40	9.7	53.1
1989	1.07	9.5	0.14	2.03	8.4	64.8
1990	0.85	7.8	0.17	2.52	7.3	43.7
1991	0.79	7.4	0.14	1.84	7.1	39.4

Source: Derived from figures in IMF, *International Financial Statistics.*
Note: Figures are for intracommodity, year-by-year comparisons only. Data cannot be used to compare changes in terms of trade for one commodity versus another.

followed by a significant decline in the terms of trade while the accord of 1983 saw a temporary firming of prices (Table 3.14). Similarly, of the ICCAs of 1976, 1981, and 1986, only the first resulted in higher prices. Since 1986, the relative price of cocoa has declined by over 87 percent from its peak value in 1977. Finally, the Natural Rubber Agreement of 1980 was followed by two years of significant price declines. Thus whether prices are measured in absolute or relative terms, cartels have done little to assist exporters.

CARTELS AND COMMODITY FUTURES TRADING

In addition to the variations of supply and demand, markets for raw materials are impacted by trading on futures and options exchanges. That a proportion of these transactions are purely speculative suggests that trading may contribute to volatility. Bosworth and Lawrence (1982, 86–87) had set out to prove that such speculation added to price volatility, particularly during the 1970s, yet they found that the empirical evidence contradicted their original assumptions. Their work demonstrated that the addition of commodities to existing holdings of stocks and bonds actually increased investor risk. It has become apparent that futures markets, which are part of the major commodity exchanges, are a potential source of stability for producers. There is now substantial research to support the notion that futures markets are reliable forecasters of forward prices. It is therefore unlikely that futures and options trading contributes to market volatility. Moreover, futures contracts represent the assumption of risk by speculators on behalf of producers. Under these circumstances, it is likely that commodity exporters will benefit from the existence of organized, efficient forward markets.

It was McKinnon (1967) who first argued that futures markets provide primary producers with a means of securing a known future price. Later, Gilbert (1985) argued that collusive agreements and futures contracts perform the same function and are therefore redundant. Measuring the risk benefits from cartelization both with and without futures markets in place, Gilbert concluded that in the presence of efficient futures markets, the producers of cocoa, coffee, sugar, and tin—like those for the noncartelized commodities of copper, cotton, rice, and tea—suffer financially when cartels are formed. A similar indictment of cartels was presented by Gemill (1985), who examined the risk benefits of both buffer stocks and forward trading for cocoa, coffee, and sugar for the period from 1961 to 1978.[2] Gemill's model firmly supported the use of futures contracts over buffer stocks as a means of reducing risk in the international sugar market. The findings for the cocoa and coffee markets were, on the other hand, ambiguous. Although the use of futures markets tended to be more cost-effective than buffer stocks for the cocoa producers, neither mechanism achieved the level of risk reduction necessary to make it attractive to exporters. As for coffee, forward trading provided superior risk reduction in three of the six exporters examined. In contrast to the positions held by Gilbert and Gemill, MacBean and Nguyen (1987) argued that futures markets are imperfect and that speculation influences future prices. Moreover, the latter authors noted that futures contracts have a very limited timeframe, for, in general, they cannot be used for planning beyond a six-month horizon.

Futures Trading on the New York Coffee, Sugar, and Cocoa Exchange

Price data for the New York Coffee, Sugar, and Cocoa Exchange (CSCE) in the 1970s provides substantial evidence that futures markets influence overall trade conditions for commodities. As detailed by Bosworth and Lawrence (1982, 84), pending futures contracts can represent sev-

Table 3.15

Commodity Futures Contracts for Coffee and Cocoa, 1974–1996 (in thousands of contracts and as a percentage of total world output)

| | Coffee "C" | | Cocoa | |
Year	(Contracts)	(%)	(Contracts)	(%)
1974	151.9	68.9	469.7	324.4
1975	71.1	24.6	426.9	276.0
1976	174.5	67.3	453.6	300.4
1977	214.2	99.7	418.5	312.5
1978	164.0	65.5	303.0	200.4
1979	449.8	161.5	315.8	210.3
1980	906.9	313.7	456.5	276.5
1981	515.3	169.2	562.7	332.2
1982	556.4	160.7	608.0	350.0
1983	427.4	147.9	1,162.5	752.4
1984	499.1	159.2	1,127.8	730.0
1985	650.8	204.0	800.6	407.0
1986	1,073.1	317.4	777.8	399.7
1987	964.6	344.2	895.5	444.6
1988	1,149.7	315.6	1,268.1	572.8
1989	1,329.0	399.7	1,341.9	543.1
1990	1,774.1	518.2	1,635.9	676.3
1991	1,772.6	501.2	1,233.5	488.3
1992	2,152.4	588.1	1,397.2	607.2
1993	2,489.2	759.1	2,128.4	881.0
1994	2,658.1	807.2	2,417.0	959.5
1995	2,003.0	577.9	2,090.1	871.6
1996	2,039.6	642.8	2,121.6	737.7

Source: CRB, *Commodity Yearbook.*

Note: Traditionally, coffee contracts have been sold on the CSCE (each contract representing 37,500 pounds or 17 metric tons of beans). Cocoa is traded on the same exchange, with each contract representing 22,000 pounds or 10 metric tons. More recently, coffee and cocoa have also been traded on the London Mercantile Exchange.

eral years of consumption for a commodity, a finding that suggests that speculation is more important than actual demand. For example, they demonstrated that as a percentage of total demand for cocoa, the turnover in contracts rose from 242 percent in 1972 to 373 percent by 1980. Similarly, whereas coffee contracts represented only 3 percent of end-use in 1972, by 1980 they translated into 433 percent of demand. The same was true for sugar futures, which rose from 46 to 220 percent of total demand during the same period. Not surprisingly, this increased level of activity on commodity exchanges persisted into the 1980s. Tables 3.15 and 3.16 show the volume of contracts traded on the cocoa, coffee,

Table 3.16

Commodity Futures Contracts for Petroleum and Sugar, 1974–1996 (in thousands of contracts and as a percentage of total world output)

Year	Petroleum (Contracts)	Petroleum (%)	Sugar (Contracts)	Sugar (%)
1974	—	—	736.9	46.5
1976	—	—	984.7	61.1
1977	—	—	1,056.0	61.7
1978	—	—	1,016.8	56.1
1975	—	—	790.6	51.1
1979	—	—	1,792.7	101.0
1980	—	—	3,576.7	214.9
1981	—	—	2,470.3	141.9
1982	—	—	2,037.0	102.9
1983	323.2	1.6	3,202.0	160.5
1984	1,840.3	9.2	2,449.5	130.2
1985	3,980.9	19.8	3,012.9	156.9
1986	8,313.5	40.0	3,583.8	184.3
1987	14,581.6	69.1	3,853.5	188.3
1988	18,858.9	86.6	5,819.1	284.8
1989	20,534.9	92.6	6,243.4	300.5
1990	23,686.9	105.5	5,424.8	253.4
1991	21,005.9	94.2	4,268.5	191.1
1992	21,109.6	94.7	3,667.5	159.9
1993	24,868.6	109.3	4,285.9	194.2
1994	26,812.3	117.9	4,719.2	218.4
1995	23,614.0	102.3	4,711.1	206.6
1996	23,487.8	99.3	4,751.9	197.0

Source: CRB, *Commodity Yearbook.*
Note: Crude oil futures are traded on the New York Mercantile Exchange, with each contract representing 1,000 barrels of oil. Sugar is traded on the CSCE, with each contract representing 112,000 pounds (approximately 50.9 metric tons) of #11 sugar, by far the largest category (the volume of trade for #14 sugar was just under 4 percent of that for #11 sugar in 1996).

petroleum, and sugar markets in New York from 1974 through 1996, both in units and as a percentage of total production.

The number of coffee contracts traded on the CSCE in 1974 was equivalent to just under 70 percent of total world production. The annual turnover in contracts continued to represent less than annual output until 1979, when 162 percent of total coffee production was traded. A decade later, futures trading was equal to nearly 400 percent of supply, a figure that continued to rise until 1994, when the contracts traded totaled 807 percent of production. These numbers suggest that speculation in coffee now accounts for more of the commodity than the market itself. One of the primary elements determining the volume of futures contracts is the presence of a functioning ICA. As will be discussed later in this chapter, the volume of futures trading is inversely related to the existence and efficiency of a cartel within the given market.

While futures contracts in coffee did not exceed total production until the late 1970s, cocoa contracts were already 324 percent of total output by 1974. This high level of futures trading was likely due to the greater variability in cocoa prices, which encourages the use of futures markets for both securing a predictable price and engaging in speculation. The ratio of turnover to total cocoa production was relatively stable until 1983, when it suddenly doubled to 752 percent of output. As will be argued below, much of this increased participation in the cocoa futures markets is attributable to the failure of the ICCA of 1981 and the ensuing market volatility. Although the volume of contracts declined somewhat in 1985 and 1986, it subsequently rebounded until by 1994 futures contracts represented nearly 950 percent of world production.

Trading in sugar futures has remained much more placid, with total contracts representing just 197 percent of production in 1996. As discussed above, the international sugar market is considerably more dispersed than other commodity markets, with many more producing and importing nations. This dispersion has tended to reduce price variability and limit the need for futures contracts. Even with the increased volatility in prices in the 1970s, the volume of trading remained below world production until 1979. It was only during the period from 1988 to 1990 that speculation took place, with contracts representing from 250 to 300 percent of world supply.

Options Trading on the New York Coffee, Sugar, and Cocoa Exchange

When examining the trading of coffee, cocoa, and sugar on the CSCE, one must also consider options contracts, which are a near-perfect substitute for futures contracts. Although futures contracts were a common means of reducing risk during the 1970s, options did not begin to play a significant role in most commodity markets until the mid-1980s. Table 3.17 illustrates the volume of options contracts for coffee and cocoa from 1986 through 1996. In 1986, coffee options represented less than 2 percent of world production, whereas the volume of futures contracts stood at over 300 percent of output. Likewise, in the cocoa market, options trading reflected less than 1 percent of annual supply, whereas the volume of futures contracts was approximately 800 percent of production.

Table 3.17

Commodity Options Contracts for Coffee and Cocoa, 1986–1996 (in thousands of contracts and as a percentage of total world output)

Year	Coffee "C" (Contracts)	(%)	Cocoa (Contracts)	(%)
1974	5.3	1.6	1.0	0.5
1987	25.6	9.2	13.9	6.9
1988	65.2	18.4	95.5	43.1
1989	114.2	34.0	153.6	62.2
1990	282.6	82.5	344.9	142.6
1991	411.6	116.8	163.6	64.9
1992	860.9	236.3	209.9	91.2
1993	1022.0	312.2	326.8	135.3
1994	1208.9	367.6	341.1	135.4
1995	867.3	250.5	319.5	133.2
1996	856.7	270.3	335.2	116.6

Source: CRB, *Commodity Yearbook.*

Note: Coffee and cocoa options are traded on the CSCE. As with futures contracts, each coffee option represents 37,500 pounds of coffee, while cocoa options represent 10 metric tons each.

By the mid-1990s, options had become a much more widely used means of securing price stability. The ratio of contracts to production for both coffee and cocoa peaked in 1994, with volume representing, respectively, 367 percent and 135 percent of production. Not surprisingly, the number of futures contracts for these commodities also attained its highest level. Table 3.18 and Figure 3.5 contain figures for futures and options contracts for both coffee and cocoa for selected years. In 1994, the aggregate volume of trading represented ten times the yearly production of these products. The numbers support the assertion that futures and options markets provide the means for securing known prices and therefore can serve as substitutes for cartelization. Indeed, when the ICA forged in 1975 was finally put into effect in 1980, the volume of futures and options contracts, which had been running at nearly 300 percent of world production, dropped to just 161 percent of output by 1982. Following the renewal of the ICA in 1983, the volume of coffee contracts dipped slightly but then gradually rebounded to over 300 percent by 1989, the year in which the accord expired; these numbers reveal the relative ineffectiveness of this accord. Nonetheless, after its expiration, the volume of trading skyrocketed to over 600 percent of production by 1990.

A somewhat similar pattern can be observed for the cocoa agreements, which were signed in 1976, 1981, and 1986.[3] As illustrated in

Table 3.18

Aggregate Volume of Futures and Options Contracts for Coffee and Cocoa for Selected Years (in thousands of contracts and as a percentage of total world output)

Year	Coffee "C" (Contracts)	(%)	Cocoa (Contracts)	(%)
1980	**906.9**	**313.7**	**456.5**	**276.5**
1982	**556.4**	**160.7**	**608.0**	**350.0**
1984	**499.1**	**159.2**	**1127.8**	**730.0**
1986	1078.4	319.0	778.8	573.3
1988	1214.9	334.0	1363.6	615.9
1990	2056.7	600.7	1980.8	818.9
1992	3013.3	824.4	1607.1	698.4
1994	3867.0	1174.8	2758.1	1094.9
1996	2896.3	913.1	2456.8	854.3

Note: Bold figures represent years in which only futures contracts are relevant. Numbers are derived from Tables 3.15 and 3.17.

Figure 3.5   **Volume of Coffee, Cocoa, and Sugar Contracts**

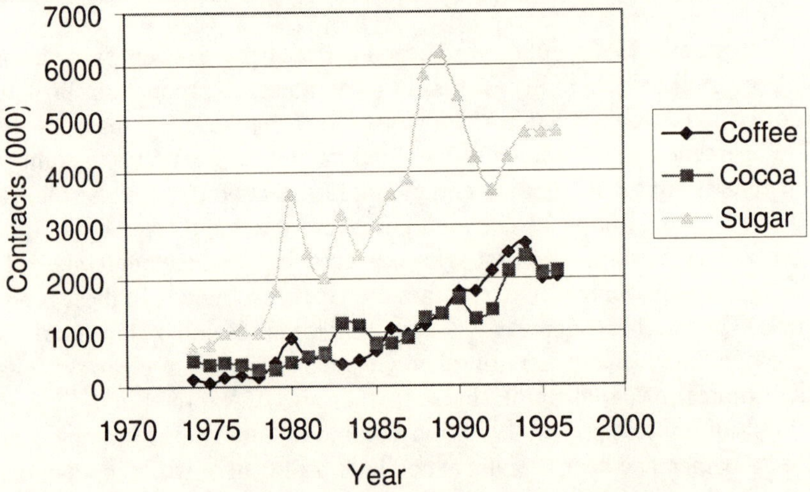

Table 3.18, these ICCAs tended to temporarily reduce the volume of futures and options contracts, with an approximate 33 percent reduction experienced between 1976 and 1978, and a 21 percent decline between 1984 and 1986. The 1981 agreement did little to affect supply, prices, or futures markets, as the nonparticipation of Ghana in this ICCA led to the immediate failure of the accord.

A similar pattern of options trading occurred in the petroleum and

Table 3.19

Commodity Options Contracts for Petroleum and Sugar, 1983–1996 (in thousands of contracts and as a percentage of total world output)

Year	Petroleum (Contracts)	(%)	Sugar (Contracts)	(%)
1984	—	—	12.0	0.6
1985	—	—	91.4	4.8
1986	135.3	0.6	24.5	13.1
1987	3,117.0	14.9	432.9	21.2
1988	5,480.3	25.1	1,536.3	75.3
1989	5,686.0	25.7	1,932.8	93.2
1990	5,254.6	23.5	2393.0	112.0
1991	4,968.7	22.4	1,513.0	67.9
1992	6,562.2	29.4	848.8	37.1
1993	7,156.5	32.1	916.2	41.6
1994	5,675.1	25.0	1,166.7	54.1
1995	3,975.6	17.2	1,203.8	52.9
1996	5,271.5	22.3	1,094.8	45.5

Note: Crude oil options are traded on the New York Mercantile Exchange. Each contract represents 1,000 barrels of oil. Sugar options are traded on the CSCE. Each contract represents 112,000 pounds (approximately 50.9 metric tons) of sugar.

Figure 3.6   **Options Contracts for Coffee, Cocoa, Sugar, and Petroleum**

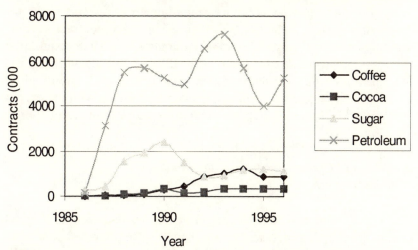

sugar markets (Table 3.19 and Figure 3.6). When OPEC effectively collapsed in 1986—with petroleum prices falling to their lowest levels in 13 years—it became apparent that an alternative mechanism for achieving price stability was needed. While petroleum options trading was minimal in 1986, representing only 0.6 percent of total production, it

Table 3.20

Aggregate Volume of Futures and Options Contracts for Petroleum and Sugar for Selected Years (in thousands of contracts and as a percentage of total world output)

Year	Petroleum (Contracts)	(%)	Sugar (Contracts)	(%)
1984	**1,840.3**	**9.2**	2,461.5	130.8
1986	8,448.8	40.6	3,838.3	197.4
1988	24,339.2	111.7	7,355.4	360.1
1990	28,941.5	129.0	7,817.8	365.4
1992	27,671.8	124.1	4,516.3	197.0
1994	32,487.4	142.9	5,885.9	272.5
1996	28,759.3	121.6	5,846.7	242.5

Note: Bold figures represent years in which only futures contracts are relevant. Numbers are derived from Tables 3.16 and 3.19.

rose rapidly thereafter, reaching 25 percent of total world supply by 1988. Similarly, sugar options represented only 0.4 percent of production in 1983, but rose precipitously to 112 percent by 1990.

The combined volume of futures and options contracts for oil and sugar is illustrated in Table 3.20. The direct link between a functioning cartel and contract volume is most apparent in the figures for petroleum. Indeed, when OPEC faltered in 1986, contract volume rose significantly, with the number of contracts in 1988 standing at 1223 percent over those for 1984. With OPEC unable to control prices, free markets took over the task of pricing petroleum. It is difficult to reach any conclusions regarding the sugar market, for with the exception of the 1977 accord, the ISAs predate the active futures and options markets.

Futures and Options Trading on the London Mercantile Exchange

The figures presented so far represent trading on markets in the United States. The London Mercantile Exchange has also offered contracts for cocoa (since 1929), coffee (beginning in 1958), and sugar (since 1983). Thus aggregate worldwide volume is actually greater than that reflected in Table 3.18. The importance of the London exchange in relation to the futures and options markets in New York is illustrated in Table 3.21. Although the volume of contracts for sugar remained small in London,

Table 3.21

Contract Volume on the London Mercantile Exchange as a Percentage of Trading on the New York CSCE, 1989–1996

Year	Sugar	Cocoa	Coffee
1989	5.4	115.8	—
1990	6.4	104.5	—
1991	7.3	124.6	—
1992	8.3	100.0	40.7
1993	7.7	89.6	36.5
1994	10.2	66.2	47.8
1995	12.2	79.1	53.1
1996	12.2	79.6	58.0

Source: CRB, *Commodity Yearbook.*

trading in cocoa futures exceeded the volume in New York for much of this period. Coffee contracts originating on the London exchange also represented a significant addition to total trading. Combining the information compiled in Table 3.21 with the figures already presented on U.S. contracts indicates that the total volume of trading in the London and New York exchanges was approximately 15 times production in 1996. Although it might seem that this magnitude of speculative purchases would destabilize international markets, the evidence indicates that futures markets are accurate forecasters of forward prices.

A Nontraditional Futures Exchange—The International Rubber Market

In contrast to the well-established futures markets (for cocoa, coffee, petroleum, and sugar), the trading of natural rubber in Japan is relatively recent (other commodities traded on newer exchanges include robusto coffees [Budapest], peanuts [Beijing], and corn [Tokyo]). The long-term cartelization of the rubber market made futures contracts unnecessary, and so it was not until 1986, when the collusive agreement was weak, that significant trading began. Table 3.22 illustrates the volume of rubber contracts on Japan's KOBE Rubber Exchange (KRE) and the Tokyo Commodity Exchange (TOCOM). Volume on the KRE rose from 1.146 million contracts in 1989 to 2.233 million contracts in 1996, an increase of approximately 95 percent. Volume on the TOCOM increased 294 percent during this period, from approximately 2.305 to 9.085 million contracts. The dominant role played by the Japanese exchanges can be attributed to the size of the automo-

Table 3.22

Natural Rubber Futures Contracts on the KRE and TOCOM Exchanges, 1989–1996

Year	Sugar	Cocoa	Coffee
1989	1,145.5	2,305.6	3,451.1
1990	1,383.4	2,308.4	3,691.8
1991	1,374.3	2,167.3	3,541.6
1992	791.9	1,726.5	2,518.4
1993	1,275.1	2,973.2	4,248.3
1994	2,933.9	9,021.9	11,955.8
1995	3,810.9	14,287.8	18,098.8
1996	2,232.8	9,085.7	11,318.5

Source: CRB, Commodity Yearbook.

bile industry, for natural rubber is far superior to synthetics in the production of tires.

As detailed earlier in the chapter, the Natural Rubber Agreements of the 1980s produced only mixed results. With the 1980 agreement, target prices were maintained through significant purchases and sales of buffer stocks. Conversely, the 1987 accord was doomed to failure, for the demand for rubber—already declining after 1988—spiraled downward as the worldwide recession of the early 1990s gutted automobile sales. A recovery did not occur until 1994. As shown in Table 3.22, the volume of futures contracts rose significantly as a result of the cartel's inability to maintain prices. It is likely that futures markets will continue to regulate prices in the rubber market.

Futures and Options Trading and Variability in Prices

It is difficult to directly measure the impact of futures and options trading on price variability. As argued above, cartels and futures markets offer alternative means of securing known prices. Thus when collusive agreements are in effect, contract volume is low and prices remain stable. Conversely, in markets where cartels are nonexistent or ineffective, suppliers and consumers protect themselves from price volatility by purchasing futures and options contracts. The widespread assumption that futures trading causes price instability is misleading. Rather, the numbers suggest that greater price variability is the natural accompaniment to increased contract volume, and hence there is no causality.

The tangential relationship between contract volume and monthly price variations for four key commodities is demonstrated in Table 3.23. Increased trading on the coffee exchange, for example, was accompanied by greater price variability in only two years, 1994 and 1996. In fact, as the contract volume doubled between 1986 and 1990, the coefficient of variation for prices fell by 60 percent. Moreover, decreased trading in 1996 was accompanied by greater market volatility. An erratic pattern is evident in the rubber market, for whereas the inception of futures trading in 1990 was initially accompanied by a reduction in price variability, one detects a direct correlation between the volume of contracts and market instability after 1994. Any suggestion of causality between futures trading and price variations is completely disproved in the sugar market, where a near tripling of trading volume occurred between 1984 and 1990, yet the coefficient of variation remained essentially the same. By 1996, with trading activity still more than twice what it had been in 1984, the variation in prices had dropped by 75 percent. A similar disconnection between futures contract volume and price movements is apparent in the petroleum market. Under the influence of OPEC's production and pricing targets, the coefficient of variation of oil prices was only 0.012 in 1984, yet it increased twenty-fivefold by 1986, prior to the expansion of futures trading. There is no clear pattern in the variability of prices from 1988 through 1996. The numbers suggest that any connection between price instability and speculation on futures markets is weak at best. Thus the slight variation in prices and market volume observed in the coffee and rubber markets does not necessarily indicate that futures markets are destabilizing, as the causality may run from price volatility to increased market volume and not vice versa.

When Will Cartels Work Better Than Futures and Options Markets?

As noted in chapter 2, there are fundamental differences between markets for agricultural commodities such as cocoa, coffee, and sugar and those for natural resources such as bauxite, petroleum, and tin. The ultimate production levels for agricultural commodities are an unknown at the beginning of a crop cycle, since the climatic conditions that prevail may significantly affect output. In addition, although cocoa, coffee, and sugar can be stored for lengthy periods of time, excess stocks must eventually be either released into the market or destroyed. The carrying costs

Table 3.23

Contract Volume and Price Variability for Coffee, Petroleum, Rubber, and Sugar for Selected Years (in thousands)

		1984	1986	1988	1990	1992	1994	1996
Coffee	Volume	499	1,078	1215	2,057	3,013	3,867	2,896
	Variation	—	0.15	0.05	0.06	0.10	0.37	0.42
Petro.	Volume (millions)	1.8	8.4	24.3	28.9	27.7	32.5	28.8
	Variation	0.0	0.32	0.91	0.31	0.09	0.13	0.10
Rubber	Volume	0.1	—	—	3,692	2,518	11,956	11,319
	Variation		0.05	0.09	0.02	0.03	0.19	0.23
Sugar	Volume	2462	3,839	7,355	7,818	4,516	5,886	5,847
	Variation	0.19	0.18	0.16	0.18	0.09	0.10	0.05

Note: Price variability is measured as the coefficient of variation of average monthly prices.

Table 3A-1

Concentration Ratios for Key Commodities (as percentages)

Commodity	Year	Concentration Ratio
Bauxite	1995	70.3
Cocoa	1997	72.1
Coffee	1997	51.9
Manganese	1995	64.4
Petroleum	1996	38.0
Rubber	1994	81.3
Sugar	1997	36.0
Tin	1995	69.3
Tungsten	1995	88.8

Source: CRB, Commodity Yearbook.

Table 3A-2

Concentration Ratios for Key Commodities, 1974 (as percentages)

Commodity	Concentration Ratio
Bauxite	54.6
Cocoa	70.4
Coffee	46.2
Manganese	—
Petroleum	57.8
Sugar	33.9
Tin	65.3
Tungsten	57.9

Source: CRB, Commodity Yearbook.

of maintaining buffer stocks in these commodities can be significant. Conversely, suppliers of minerals can easily speed up or slow down production in response to changes in demand. Consequently, cooperation on production could eliminate the need for (and costs of) buffer stocks.

The intrinsic differences between agricultural commodities and natural resources indicate that cartels may, in fact, offer a superior approach to managing prices for producers of materials such as bauxite, petroleum, and tin. In the absence of uncertainties about final production, target prices can be easily maintained without reliance on buffer stocks. The matching of supply and demand requires a degree of cooperation among producers that has rarely been attained.[4] The collapse of the International Tin Agreement in 1985 is but one example of the tendency of cartel members to increase output at the risk of flooding the market with a commodity that is already in excess supply. Thus although collusive agreements may be preferred to futures markets for producers of material resources, their success requires significant sacrifices on the part of cartel members.

CONCLUSION

The cartelization of markets was a poor solution to the problem of declining and unstable commodity prices. As discussed above, most of the collusive agreements reached since 1960 have failed to meet at least one of the requisite criteria for a successful cartel: limited membership, nonsubstitutability, barriers to entry, nonperishability, and homogeneity of the product. Consequently, while cartels have temporarily affected world prices and production, the intrinsic characteristics of each commodity market eventually doomed the arrangements.

The attractiveness of cartelization to both commodity exporters and international agencies such as UNCTAD appears to be waning. With the exception of the bauxite cartel, no collusive arrangements have succeeded in permanently stabilizing prices in the commodity markets of developing nations. As will be argued in chapter 5, it is time for commodity producers to seek an alternative means of achieving a degree of control over the price they receive for their exports.

NOTES

1. Unlike other cartel arrangements, the International Rubber Agreement allowed for a great deal of discretion on the part of the buffer stock manager. Four price barriers were set: "may-sell," "must-sell," "may-buy," and "must-buy." As Burger and Smit noted (1990, 718), considerable buying occurred in the first seven years of the agreement in spite of the fact that the price never entered the "must-buy" or "must-sell" ranges.

2. Gemill's rejection of buffer stocks as a means of reducing risk is even more compelling when one considers the bias against forward markets that he built into his model (1985, 415).

3. One must keep in mind that the ICCAs were never effective in managing world cocoa prices. Consequently, it would not be surprising that futures contracts were popular even when an ICCA was in place.

4. The manipulation of output is especially difficult in agricultural markets. The situation is very different for oil producers, who can curtail output by merely turn-

ing a spigot. Thus when the members of OPEC managed to agree to significant production quotas in April 1999, the new quotas were acted on expeditiously and prices jumped.

REFERENCES

Anderson, R., and Gilbert, C. 1988. "Commodity Agreements and Commodity Markets: Lessons from Tin." *Economic Journal* 98: 1–15.

Balassa, B. 1964. *Trade Prospects for Developing Countries*. Homewood, IL: Irwin.

Bosworth, B., and Lawrence, R. 1982. *Commodity Prices and the New Inflation*. Washington, DC: Brookings Institution.

Burger, K., and Smit, H. 1990. "Long-Term and Short-Term Analysis of the Natural Rubber Market." *Weltwirtschaftliches Archives* 125, no. 4: 718–747.

Gemill, G. 1985. "Forward Contracts or International Buffer Stocks? A Study of Their Relative Efficiencies in Stabilizing Commodity Export Earnings." *Economic Journal* 95: 400–417.

Ghanem, S. 1986. *OPEC: The Rise and Fall of an Exclusive Club*. London: Routledge.

Gilbert, C. 1985. "Futures Trading and the Welfare Evaluation of Commodity Price Stabilization." *Economic Journal* 95: 637–661.

———. 1987. "International Commodity Agreements: Design and Performance." *World Development* 15, no. 5: 591–616.

Herrmann, R.; Burger, K.; and Smit, H. 1993. *International Commodity Policy*. London: Routledge.

Hillman, John. 1988. "Malaya and the International Tin Cartel." *Modern Asian Studies* 22, no. 2: 237–261.

Holloway, S. 1988. *The Aluminum Multinationals and the Bauxite Cartel*. New York: St. Martin's Press.

MacBean, A., and Nguyen, D. 1987. "International Commodity Agreements: Shadow and Substance." *World Development* 15: 575–590.

McKinnon, R. 1967. "Futures Markets, Buffer Stocks, and Income Stability for Primary Producers." *Journal of Political Economy* 75: 844–861.

Spar, D. 1994. *The Cooperative Edge*. Ithaca: Cornell University Press.

Stocking, G., and Watkins, M. 1991. *Cartels in Action: Case Studies in International Business Diplomacy*. Buffalo: Business Enterprises Reprint Series.

4

The Impact of Commodity Price Inflation on the Developed Nations

When the topics of commodity prices and cartels have been addressed in the literature, they have generally been treated in terms of the economic consequences for the developing nations rather than the disruptions experienced by the industrialized world. The general rise in the price of commodities that took place from 1970 to 1982 resulted in slow economic growth, high unemployment, and accelerating inflation for the developed countries. Most of these effects can be traced back to the twentyfold increase in the price of petroleum engineered by OPEC between 1971 and 1979. The inability of the developed nations to effectively substitute alternative energy resources for petroleum in the near term left them particularly vulnerable to price hikes. During this period, the consuming countries also bore the brunt of price increases for other commodities, including critical minerals such as tin and alumina, as well as cocoa, coffee, sugar, and their derivative products.

Indeed, the late 1970s inaugurated an unprecedented period of commodity inflation that rocked the economic foundations of the industrialized world.[1] As noted in chapter 3, the patterns of price increases across the various commodity products are remarkably similar. With the exception of petroleum, most commodity prices were stable until just after 1975, when they rose dramatically until the abrupt corrections of the early 1980s. Prices then began to erode, essentially returning to the levels of 1975 by the mid-1980s. For example, tin sold for approximately $6,900 per metric ton in 1975, climbing to a peak over $16,700 per ton by 1980, but by 1986, the price had returned to just over $6,000 per ton. Similarly, natural rubber sold for $658 per ton in 1975, rising by nearly 150 percent to $1,600 per ton in 1980, before prices began to decline, falling to $920 per ton in 1985, a decline of over 42 percent in five years. Cocoa prices were also at their weakest in 1975, when a metric ton sold for just $1,245. Prices rose rapidly to over $4,000 per ton in 1977 before falling precipitously to $1,500 per ton in 1982. Owing to the implementation of the conciliatory coffee accords in the 1970s, the fluctuations in prices for that commodity were less erratic. Although coffee reached a peak price of $319 per 60-kilogram bag in 1977, prices then began a somewhat orderly retreat, and with the exception of a significant increase in 1986, they continued to drop until hitting a low of $84 per bag in 1992.

The first section of this chapter will examine the widespread economic impact that the price increases of the 1970s had on the developed world. Emphasis will be placed on the role played by key commodities—including bauxite (alumina), petroleum, rubber, and tin—in specific U.S. industries. The effect that rising cocoa and coffee prices had on U.S. consumers will also be discussed. It will be shown that the price instabilities of commodity markets in the 1970s and early 1980s imposed hardships on both the consuming nations in the industrialized world and the developing nations responsible for the products. As will be argued in chapter 5, it is in the best interests of both producers and consumers of commodities to strive for cooperative measures that will prevent future market disruptions.

ECONOMIC CONDITIONS IN THE INDUSTRIALIZED COUNTRIES IN THE 1970S

Beginning with petroleum, the rapid increase in the prices of imported commodities in the 1970s resulted in a fundamental change in economic conditions in the United States, Japan, and Western Europe. Until this time, inflation had not been a significant problem in the developed world. Moreover, unemployment levels had remained low throughout the 1950s and 1960s, with occasional temporary increases attributable to recessionary stages of the business cycle.

Rising Oil Prices and the Consumer Price Index

The rapid rise in petroleum prices that OPEC orchestrated beginning in 1973 introduced a spate of inflation in the industrialized nations. Indeed, whereas the change in the U.S. Consumer Price Index (CPI) was a

Table 4.1

Changes in Consumer Prices for Seven Industrialized Nations, 1970–1988

Year	U.S.	Japan	Germany	France	U.K.	Italy	Canada
1970	5.8	7.3	3.4	5.8	6.2	5.2	3.5
1971	4.3	6.4	5.3	5.6	9.5	4.7	2.8
1972	3.3	4.9	5.5	6.0	6.9	5.9	4.8
1973	6.1	11.6	7.1	7.3	9.4	10.3	7.7
1974	11.6	24.1	7.2	14.5	16.8	20.4	11.4
1975	8.6	11.0	5.7	10.9	23.3	16.3	10.3
1976	5.7	9.3	4.3	9.7	16.5	16.4	7.5
1977	6.5	8.2	3.7	9.4	15.9	19.4	8.0
1978	7.6	4.2	2.7	9.3	8.2	12.3	8.9
1979	11.3	3.7	4.1	10.6	13.4	15.7	9.2
1980	13.6	7.6	5.5	13.6	18.0	21.1	10.2
1981	10.3	4.9	6.3	13.3	11.9	19.3	12.4
1982	6.1	2.7	5.3	11.9	8.6	16.4	10.8
1983	3.2	1.9	3.3	9.5	4.6	14.9	5.8
1984	4.3	2.2	2.4	7.6	5.0	10.6	4.4
1985	3.5	2.1	2.1	5.9	6.0	8.6	3.9
1986	1.9	0.6	-0.1	2.5	3.4	6.2	4.2
1987	3.7	0.1	0.2	3.3	4.2	4.6	4.4
1988	4.1	0.7	1.3	2.7	4.9	5.0	4.0

Source: IMF, *International Financial Statistics.*

modest 3.3 percent in 1972, it rose by 6.6 percent in 1973, a doubling of the inflation rate (Table 4.1). The trend accelerated in 1974, with prices rising by 11.6 percent. Although still high by historical standards, the inflation rates of the mid-1970s were modest, but the situation soon changed, and prices rose by 11.3 percent in 1979 and by 13.6 percent in 1980. OPEC's grip on the international petroleum market then began to weaken, and as oil prices slid, so did the inflation rate in the United States, dropping to 6.1 percent in 1982.

The situation was significantly worse for some of the other industrialized nations. Unlike the United States, with its significant petroleum reserves, nations such as Japan, Italy, and France were almost entirely dependent on imported oil. The rise in the inflation rate in Japan was especially severe, for with the exception of limited coal deposits, the country lacked alternative energy resources. From a rate of change of only 4.9 percent in 1972, the growth rate of Japan's CPI increased to 24.1 percent in 1974, and the downward trend in the inflation rate beginning in 1975 was considerably slower than that observed for the United

States. The severe economic dislocations caused by the inflation of oil prices led to a significant restructuring of the Japanese economy, to the extent that when the second oil price hike began in the late 1970s, the inflation rate barely budged. Japan's success in both adopting manufacturing methods that consumed significantly less oil and in developing nuclear power had paid off.

Of the European economies, the British and Italian were the hardest hit by the inflation of the 1970s. In Great Britain, the inflation rate rose from 6.9 percent in 1972 to 23.3 percent in 1975. Moreover, with the exception of 1978, the CPI grew by double digits in every year from 1974 to 1981, and prices nearly tripled. Similar to the situation in the United States, inflation in Great Britain was largely under control by the mid-1980s, when the CPI grew in the range of 4 to 5 percent per year. The economic disruptions were even more severe in Italy, where the CPI rose over 10 percent in 1973 and double-digit inflation persisted for twelve years, hitting a peak of 21.1 percent in 1980. The cumulative effect of this sustained period of inflation was a nearly fivefold increase in prices by 1984. Italy's inflation rate remained above that for the other major industrialized nations throughout the remainder of the 1980s.

Stagflation and the Industrialized Economies

The most vexing aspect of the inflation of the 1970s and early 1980s was the fact that it coincided with declining growth rates and rising unemployment in the industrialized world to create so-called stagflation. Table 4.2 illustrates the growth in industrial production for the seven major industrial powers for the period from 1972 to 1988. By 1975, rising inflation rates were accompanying a downturn in industrial production. The exception to this was France, which did not experience declines until 1976, with recovery occurring in the next year. The acceleration of inflation around 1980 was once again accompanied by declining industrial output in United States, Canada, the United Kingdom, Germany, and France. It was not until inflation declined after 1982 that the G-7 nations experienced rapid and sustained economic growth.

The decline in growth rates in the 1970s resulted in rising unemployment for most of the nations of the industrialized world. As illustrated in Table 4.3, the U.S. unemployment rate rose from 4.8 percent in 1973 to 8.3 percent in 1975 and then began a slow decline, but it remained above its 1973 level until the time of the second significant increase in petro-

Table 4.2

**Index of Industrial Production for Seven Industrialized Nations,
1972–1988** (1972 = 100)

Year	U.S.	Japan	Germany	France	U.K.	Italy	Canada
1970	65.3	51.9	69.2	74.0	76.7	67.3	68.9
1973	70.6	59.6	73.6	79.0	83.6	73.9	77.0
1974	69.6	57.3	73.4	82.0	81.9	76.8	78.5
1975	63.4	51.2	68.8	96.0	77.4	70.0	72.8
1976	69.3	56.9	75.1	82.0	80.0	78.5	77.6
1977	74.9	59.3	76.5	84.0	84.1	78.0	80.3
1978	79.3	63.0	78.6	86.0	86.5	79.7	83.0
1979	82.0	67.5	82.4	93.0	89.9	85.0	87.1
1980	79.7	70.6	82.6	93.0	84.0	89.4	84.1
1981	81.0	71.4	81.0	92.3	81.3	87.4	85.8
1982	76.7	71.7	78.5	91.4	82.9	84.7	77.4
1983	79.5	73.9	79.0	90.7	85.9	82.7	82.4
1984	86.6	80.7	81.2	91.2	86.0	85.4	92.4
1985	88.0	83.6	84.9	91.3	90.7	86.6	97.8
1986	89.0	83.5	86.6	91.9	92.9	90.2	96.8
1987	93.2	86.4	86.9	93.0	96.6	92.6	101.6
1988	97.4	95.3	90.3	97.3	101.2	99.1	106.9

Source: IMF, *International Financial Statistics.*

leum prices in 1979. At that point, unemployment began to rise again, reaching 7.5 percent in 1981. After 1981, when the Federal Reserve initiated a recession in the United States, the link between oil prices and economic prosperity was more tenuous, as contractionary monetary policy was instituted to reduce inflation.

In Canada, the unemployment rate rose more slowly but was more sustained than in the United States. There, joblessness stood at 5.3 percent of the labor force in 1974 and reached 8.3 percent in 1978. After a modest decline in the following three years, the onset of the 1982 recession quickly drove Canadian unemployment rates into the double digits.

The pattern was different in Europe, where unemployment rose much more slowly and never reached the levels seen in the United States and Canada. Germany's unemployment rate, for example, rose from a mere 0.8 percent in 1973 to a peak of only 3.6 percent in 1975. The economy then began a slow recovery that lasted until the 1981 recession. Italy and France also experienced only moderate increases in unemployment rates, with a recovery taking place in the early 1980s.

As for Japan, a significant drop in industrial production had little impact on the country's employment levels. In fact, it is difficult to discern any

Table 4.3

Unemployment Rates of Seven Industrialized Nations, 1972–1988 (as percentages)

Year	U.S.	Japan	Germany	France	U.K.	Italy	Canada
1972	5.5	1.4	0.5	3.0	6.2	4.0	6.3
1973	4.8	1.3	0.8	2.8	2.9	3.4	5.5
1974	5.5	1.4	1.7	3.0	2.9	2.8	5.3
1975	8.3	1.9	3.6	4.3	4.1	3.2	6.9
1976	7.6	2.0	3.6	4.7	5.5	3.6	7.1
1977	6.9	2.0	3.6	5.0	6.2	3.4	8.1
1978	6.0	2.3	3.4	5.4	6.2	3.7	8.3
1979	5.8	2.1	3.0	6.1	5.6	3.9	7.4
1980	7.0	2.0	2.9	6.5	7.0	3.9	7.5
1981	7.5	2.2	4.1	7.7	10.5	4.3	7.5
1982	9.5	2.4	5.9	8.7	12.2	4.8	11.0
1983	9.5	2.7	7.3	8.8	13.4	5.2	11.9
1984	7.4	2.8	7.1	10.0	11.8	5.9	11.2
1985	7.1	2.6	7.2	10.4	11.2	6.0	10.5
1986	6.9	2.8	6.6	10.6	11.2	7.5	9.5
1987	6.1	2.9	6.3	10.7	10.3	7.9	8.8
1988	5.6	2.5	6.3	10.2	8.6	7.9	7.8

Source: U.S. Department of Commerce, *Statistical Abstract of the United States.* Washington, DC: U.S. Government Printing Office.

pattern in Japanese unemployment, other than a structural rise that appears to be taking place over the longer term. The damage done to Japan's economy seems to have taken the form of accelerated inflation rates.

Estimating the Impact of the Oil Shocks

Numerous attempts have been made to estimate the overall effect that petroleum price shocks have had on the economies of the industrialized world. Fried and Schultze (1975, 16) projected the impact that oil priced at $10 per barrel by OPEC would have on the imports, exports, and growth rates of the developed nations. They surmised that the increased price of petroleum would decrease real aggregate demand in the United States by $13.0 billion in 1975 and by $18.1 billion in 1977. In Western Europe, the decline was expected to be $34.3 billion by 1974 and, even with conservation measures in place, $25.2 billion by 1977. Similarly, in Japan, the impact on aggregate demand was projected to fall from $12.5 billion in 1974 to $10.4 billion by 1977. As a result of the rise in their export earnings, oil-producing countries were expected to significantly increase their imports from the developed world. For the United States, this rise in exports was supposed to result in a $10.1 billion increase in GDP by 1977. Conversely, U.S. exports to developing nations without oil reserves were expected to fall, resulting in a $3.2 billion reduction in demand. For Western Europe, the trade scenario was more favorable, with increased exports to oil-producing nations raising demand by $20.6 billion and falling exports to developing nations reducing gross output by only $4.4 billion. The comparable figures for Japan were a rise of $8.7 billion in demand coupled with a reduction of $2.6 billion in the gross domestic product.

The net impact of the first oil shock for the United States was forecasted to be –$12.8 billion in 1974, falling slightly to –$11.8 billion by 1977. The initial effects on Western Europe were expected to be greater, –$29 billion in 1974, but significantly lower consumption of gasoline there resulted in a much smaller projected reduction of only $9.0 billion in 1977. Similarly, Japan was expected to have a reduction in demand of $10.5 billion in 1974, which was to fall to only $4.3 billion in 1977.

The work of Fried and Schultze has been challenged by a number of studies that examined OPEC's intervention in the world petroleum market after the fact and concluded that the rising cost of oil could only partially explain the economic disruptions of the 1970s. For example, Hickman et al. (1987) estimated that the aggregate decline in real GDP between 1973 and 1977 was 3.0 percent, a figure that drops to only 1.5 percent if one factors in the Federal Reserve's application of accommodative monetary policy.[2] Darby (1982, 749) observed that the rise in inflation rates after 1973 was greatest in nations that were in the process of removing wage-price controls, a finding that suggests that such policy changes led to the stagflation of the 1970s. Examining the oil price hike of 1973–1974, Bohi (1989) found no causal relationship between rising oil prices and declining macroeconomic activity. Rather, he attributed the difficult economic conditions of the period from 1974 to 1981 to other constraints on productivity and output such as rigid labor markets and inadequate levels of investment spending.

As discussed in chapter 3, some of the negative effects of commodity price inflation have been attributed to market volatility. In their report to the president in 1978, the Council of Economic Advisors concluded that price volatility played a significant role in reducing output. Conversely, a later governmental study of the domestic economy posited that the net impact of volatile energy prices in the United States was the reduction of real GDP by \$2.5 billion per year, a negligible change in output that suggests that price volatility played only a small role in the economic stagnation of the 1970s (U.S. Department of Energy, 1986).

Using a model to analyze how the OPEC-driven price shocks affected wages, prices, and real output for the U.S. economy, Pindyck and Rotemberg (1984, 116–117) concluded that the impact depended on the price elasticity of energy demand and the degree of rigidity in the labor market. They theorized that it is possible for output to fall only slightly, since the resulting inflation may not be accompanied by rising nominal wages (leading to lower real wages). Similarly, if energy is price-inelastic, the effect on output will be smaller. Pindyck and Rotemberg's work demonstrated that by changing the assumptions of a neoclassical model, one can arrive at significantly different results.

WITH THEIR BACKS TO THE WALL: RESPONSES TO PETROLEUM INFLATION IN THE INDUSTRIALIZED WORLD

The Strategic Petroleum Reserves of the United States

The dramatic increase in oil prices engineered by OPEC in the 1970s caused the industrialized nations to seek antidotes for market instabilities and supply disruptions. In 1975, the U.S. Energy Policy and Conservation Act (EPCA) authorized the establishment of the Strategic Petroleum Reserve (SPR), a stockpile targeted at approximately 1 billion barrels of oil—about six months worth of imports by the day's standard. Unlike accumulations of other strategic materials (e.g., tin and manganese), the primary purpose of the SPR is not to ensure the availability of inputs during armed conflict but rather to provide a safeguard against peacetime market fluctuations. The physical limits of the reserve would prevent any release of oil from being effective beyond the short term. The belief, however, was that supply interruptions would be of short duration—similar to the OPEC embargo of 1973. Plummer (1984) discussed the financing of the SPR and stressed that in order to be an effective stabilization tool, the stock would need to be drawn down before oil market disruptions occur.

As implemented by the EPCA, the oil was stored in abandoned salt mines, a tactic that initially limited the storage capacity of the project to only 248 million barrels (Sweetnam 1982, 93). The federal government continued to acquire additional salt mines, but the storage limit of these subterranean facilities stood at only 400 million barrels by the mid-1980s, a figure that was still well below target levels. By March 1995, the Strategic Petroleum Reserve's capacity had reached 750 million barrels of oil, but only 592 million barrels were in storage at that time, evidence that the gasoline lines of the 1970s were a fading memory and that the EPCA's billion-barrel storage goal was no longer an urgent priority. In an emergency, it would be possible to draw down the SPR's current store at a rate of 4.3 million barrels of oil per day, a flow that would effectively replace approximately two-thirds of U.S. daily petroleum imports for a period of 135 days. Due to the danger of gas buildup in the salt mines, however, it would be safer to limit the release of oil from the mines to 3.1 million barrels per day, which represents about 50 percent of U.S. daily imports for 190 days. If oil disruptions continued beyond six months, the holdings of the SPR would be depleted. Given the increased dispersion of petroleum production around the world, it is not clear if an OPEC-driven oil shock of the magnitude of the crisis of 1973 will occur again, but the cartel's doubling of oil prices between April and September of 1999 demonstrated a continuing ability to manipulate world production. If pushed too far, the United States might be inclined to act on a suggestion (made by New York Democratic Senator Charles Schumer in November 1999) to release significant amounts of oil from the SPR onto the market, but such a move should be made only with great caution.

Conservation and Substitution Take Hold

Heavy industry was not the only sector of the U.S. economy greatly impacted by the oil shock of 1973. In fact, across the board, domestic industries struggled to adapt to rising petroleum costs as they saw declines in their profitability. In response to this market instability, the U.S. industrial base had collectively reduced its reliance on petroleum by 1977, through either conservation measures or the use of alternative domestic energy resources (notably, natural gas).[3] The rise in consumer prices for products and services supplied by the affected industries will be examined later in this chapter.

The degree to which industries were able to either conserve petroleum or switch to an alternative source of energy varied widely. Table 4.4 illustrates the refined petroleum requirements, both absolute and as a percentage of total input expenditures, for twenty sectors of the U.S. economy in both 1972 (before the price hikes) and 1977.[4] From 1972 to 1977, the average price of a barrel of light crude oil rose from $2.80 to $12.84, a 360 percent increase, which resulted in a 183 percent increase in the price of refined petroleum inputs. That none of the sectors listed in the table experienced a rise of this magnitude in the cost of petroleum relative to other inputs suggests that a significant shift in usage had occurred by 1977. This was even the case with industries for which petroleum represented a significant percentage of inputs in 1972: "other agricultural" (5.67 percent), new construction (2.67 percent), maintenance and repair construction (7.44 percent), chemicals (2.06 percent), utilities (5.51 percent), trade (3.07 percent), and hotels and lodgings (2.49 percent). In durable manufacturing, only the stone, clay, and glass industry had a petroleum requirement high enough in 1972 to significantly affect costs (1.85 percent). In addition, only the electric, gas, and water utilities had a significant requirement for both refined and crude petroleum products (14.8 percent of total inputs).

In Table 4.5, a comparison is drawn between the proportion of total input costs attributable to oil in 1977 and projections of petroleum usage if firms had not adjusted their relative consumption. The effect was most dramatic in the fields of maintenance and repair construction and real estate, where the proportion of total expenditures attributable to petroleum declined by 67.6 percent and 84.4 percent, respectively. The sectors of miscellaneous agriculture, new construction, and food and allied products managed to reduce relative energy consumption by 46.4 percent, 46 percent, and 43.6 percent, respectively. In the service sector, hotels and lodgings reduced their projected oil utilization by over 60 percent, while transportation and warehousing, wholesale and retail trade, business services, and medical and educational services dropped their relative use of petroleum from between 35 to 50 percent. Far more modest reductions in the proportion of oil inputs to total inputs were achieved in the areas of paper and allied industries (only 12.0 percent), primary iron and steel (14.2 percent), nonferrous metals (13.1 percent), utilities (14.6 percent), and auto repair (13.4 percent).

The agricultural, construction, and service industries experienced the most dramatic drops in the utilization of petroleum products. On the other hand, with the difficulty of substituting other resources for petroleum-derived energy inputs, it is not surprising that the manufacturing sectors (SIC codes 24, 37, 38, 68, and 75) achieved

Table 4.4

Refined Petroleum Requirements for Twenty Sectors of the U.S. Economy, 1972 and 1977 (in millions of dollars and as a percentage of inputs)

SIC Code	Sector	1972		1977	
		($)	(%)	($)	(%)
01	Livestock	182	0.54	505	1.14
02	Other Agricultural	877	5.67	2,670	8.61
11	New Construction	1,995	2.67	4,771	4.08
12	Maintenance/Repair Construction	1,137	7.44	2,447	6.82
14	Food/Kindred Products	281	0.33	733	0.53
24	Paper/Allied Products	223	1.83	1108	4.56
27	Chemicals	279	2.06	1424	3.67
29	Drugs/Cleansing Preparations	100	0.97	291	1.67
36	Stone/Clay/Glass Products	147	1.85	489	3.43
37	Primary Iron/Steel	173	0.80	808	1.94
38	Primary Nonferrous Metals	112	0.62	467	1.52
65	Transportation and Warehousing	2,610	8.73	8,795	16.02
68	Electric/Gas/Water Utilities	1,370	5.51	8,099	13.32
69	Wholesale/Retail Trades	1,543	3.07	5,055	4.62
70	Finance and Insurance	157	0.46	431	0.85
71	Real Estate	447	1.33	333	0.57
72	Hotels/Lodgings	325	2.49	447	2.68
73	Business Services	395	1.84	928	2.61
75	Auto Repair Services	181	1.40	698	3.43
77	Medical/Educational Services	429	1.57	1,482	2.49

Source: U.S. Department of Commerce, *Survey of Current Business*. Washington, DC: U.S. Government Printing Office.

only modest reductions in the use of refined petroleum products. As will be shown in Table 4.9, for these industrial firms, as well as for the sectors in which the reduction in petroleum was large yet the dependence on oil remained high (SIC codes 02, 11, 12, 65, and 69), profitability was especially hurt and the need to implement conservation measures urgent.

The second oil price shock took place in 1979 when (using 1978 prices as a base) the cost of petroleum rose 126 percent in a single year. Oil

Table 4.5

Proportion of Input Costs Attributable to Petroleum: Actual Figures Versus Projections Using Fixed Input Coefficients, 1977

SIC Code	Sector	Projected	Actual	% Difference
01	Livestock	1.53	1.14	−25.5
02	Other Agricultural	16.05	8.61	−46.4
11	New Construction	7.56	4.08	−46.0
12	Maintenance/Repair Construction	21.06	6.82	−67.6
14	Food/Kindred Products	0.94	0.53	−43.6
24	Paper/Allied Products	5.18	4.56	−12.0
27	Chemicals	5.83	3.67	−37.0
29	Drugs/Cleansing	2.75	1.67	−39.3
36	Stone/Clay/Glass Products	5.24	3.43	−34.5
37	Primary Iron/Steel	2.26	1.94	−14.2
38	Primary Nonferrous Metals	1.75	1.52	−13.1
65	Transportation and Warehousing	24.71	16.02	−35.2
68	Electric/Water/Gas Utilities	15.59	13.32	−14.6
69	Wholesale/Retail Trade	8.69	4.62	−46.8
70	Finance and Insurance	1.30	0.85	−34.6
71	Real Estate	3.76	0.57	−84.8
72	Hotels/Lodgings	7.05	2.68	−62.0
73	Business Services	5.21	2.61	−49.9
75	Auto Repair Services	3.96	3.43	−13.4
77	Medical/Educational Services	4.44	2.49	−43.9

Source: Figures are derived from those presented in Table 4.4.

costs climbed an additional 57 percent between 1979 and 1980. These increases led to a 147 percent elevation in the price of refined intermediate petroleum products. The already growing trend toward reducing energy consumption accelerated, even in the sectors where demand had hardly fallen as a result of the first price hike. For a few unfortunate U.S. industries, however, the "easy" reductions in petroleum use, those achieved through changes in production techniques, had already taken place in the period between 1973 and 1978, and now further cuts in the demand for petroleum were more difficult to achieve.

THE COST OF CONTINUED DEPENDENCE ON OIL:
INDUSTRY-BY-INDUSTRY REQUIREMENTS

The demand for refined petroleum by twenty sectors of the U.S. economy for the year 1982 is presented in Table 4.6. In comparing these figures with those shown in Table 4.4, one clearly sees the increasing contribution of oil to the total input costs of the various firms. The livestock industry sector, for example, saw its expenditures on petroleum inputs rise from only 0.54 percent in 1972 to 4.23 percent in 1982. The increase was also significant for the area of miscellaneous agriculture, where oil as a percentage of total input costs rose from 5.67 percent to 12.05 percent. For the manufacturing sectors, the rise in the contribution of oil to total inputs was particularly great in the areas of paper and allied products (1.83 percent to 6.45 percent) and chemicals (2.06 percent to 5.10 percent). Several segments of the transportation and service sectors were similarly affected. For transportation and warehousing, the most energy-dependent sector of the U.S. economy, input costs attributable to oil products jumped from 8.7 percent to 19.32 percent, an increase of over 120 percent. For the sector of electric, water, and gas utilities, the number rose from 5.51 percent to 13.52 percent of expenditures. In the service sector, both wholesale and retail trade, as well as auto repair services, experienced sharp increases in their dependence on petroleum products, from 3.07 percent to 6.07 percent, and from 1.4 percent to 5.18 percent, respectively.

Some industries were not adversely affected by the second oil shock. Although relatively dependent on petroleum between 1972 and 1977, by 1982 the new construction sector had seen a slight drop in its oil requirement, from 4.08 percent to 4.02 percent of inputs. In the service sector, hotels and lodgings experienced a drop in their relative use of petroleum products from 2.49 percent to 1.74 percent of expenditures. Three additional service industries—finance and insurance, real estate, and business services—saw their reliance on petroleum inputs rise only slightly.

Table 4.7 contains the projected and actual petroleum requirements of the twenty chosen industries. Here, the coefficients have been fixed at their 1977 levels, that is, at the ratios that existed prior to the second round of price increases in 1979. The differences between the forecasted and realized input requirements for oil were smaller, in terms of percentages, than those calculated for 1977 (Table 4.5). There are several

Table 4.6

Refined Petroleum Requirements for Twenty Sectors of the U.S. Economy, 1982 (in millions of dollars and as a percentage of total inputs)

SIC Code	Sector	($)	(%)
01	Livestock	2,820	4.23
02	Other Agricultural	5,034	12.05
11	New Construction	7,044	4.02
12	Maintenance/Repair Construction	3,613	7.05
14	Food/Kindred Products	1,803	0.86
24	Paper/Allied Products	2,503	6.45
27	Chemicals	2,972	5.10
29	Drugs/Cleansing Preparations	774	2.64
36	Stone/Clay/Glass Products	881	4.67
37	Primary Iron/Steel	1,113	2.88
38	Primary Nonferrous Metals	729	7.92
65	Transportation and Warehousing	20,487	19.32
68	Electric/Gas/Water Utilities	20,709	13.52
69	Wholesale/Retail Trades	11,506	6.07
70	Finance and Insurance	1,087	1.06
71	Real Estate	828	0.88
72	Hotels/Lodgings	981	1.74
73	Business Services	2,432	3.14
75	Auto Repair Services	1,599	5.18
77	Medical/Educational Services	4,220	3.62

Source: U.S. Department of Commerce, *Survey of Current Business*.

reasons for this disparity. First, the most meaningful reductions in petroleum usage had already been achieved after the price disruption of 1973 and so further industry adjustments became more difficult after 1979. Second, while the near $20 per barrel price hike effected between 1977 and 1982 represented an increase of 153 percent, it was still relatively small compared to the 359 percent increase seen between 1972 and 1977. As a result, the market response was generally subdued.

There were some notable exceptions to this trend. For example, the new construction sector, which had already made a 46 percent reduction in projected petroleum use by 1977, saw a further reduction of 60.1 percent by 1982. Transportation and warehousing made similar reductions in expected oil consumption in response to both price hikes: a 60 percent

Table 4.7

Proportion of Input Costs Attributable to Petroleum: Actual Figures Versus Projections Using Fixed Input Coefficients, 1982

SIC Code	Sector	Projected	Actual	% Difference
01	Livestock	2.82	4.23	50.0
02	Other Agricultural	21.27	12.05	−43.3
11	New Construction	10.08	4.02	−60.1
12	Maintenance/Repair Construction	16.85	7.05	−58.2
14	Food/Kindred Products	1.31	0.86	−34.4
24	Paper/Allied Products	11.26	6.45	−42.7
27	Chemicals	9.06	5.10	−43.7
29	Drugs and Cleansing Preparations	4.12	2.64	−35.9
36	Stone/Clay/Glass Products	8.47	4.67	−44.9
37	Primary Iron/Steel	4.79	2.88	−39.8
38	Primary Nonferrous Metals	3.75	1.97	−47.5
65	Transportation and Warehousing	39.57	19.32	−51.2
68	Electric/Gas/Water Utilities	32.90	13.52	−58.9
69	Wholesale/Retail Trades	11.41	6.07	−46.8
70	Finance and Insurance	2.10	1.06	−49.5
71	Real Estate	1.41	0.88	−37.6
72	Hotels/Lodgings	6.62	1.74	−73.7
73	Business Services	6.47	3.14	−51.5
75	Auto Repair Services	8.47	5.18	−38.8
77	Medical/Educational Services	6.15	3.62	−41.1

Source: Figures are derived from Table 4.4.

reduction in the earlier period, with a drop of 51 percent in the second. The electric, gas, and water utilities, which had responded to the first oil price hike with only a modest drop in expected consumption (14.6 percent), saw a 59 percent reduction in anticipated usage following the second round of price increases. Three service sectors—hotels and lodgings, business services, and finance and insurance—experienced significant reductions in their relative use of petroleum in 1982, with demand falling below projected levels by 73.7 percent, 51.5 percent, and 49.5 percent, respectively. For industries in which petroleum does not constitute a major input expenditure, the incentive to reduce consumption was less urgent and the reduction in projected use was smaller. This was the case in the sectors of chemicals (43.7 percent reduction), real estate (37.6), and food and related products (34.4 percent).

The figures for both projected and actual petroleum use from 1972 to 1982 are shown in Table 4.8. In response to the major oil price hikes of the decade, most industries made significant overall reductions in their dependence on petroleum-based inputs: 80.5 percent for agriculture, 79.0 percent for new construction, 72.4 percent for wholesale and retail trade, 69.1 percent for transportation and warehousing, 65.8 percent for the utilities, 50.8 percent for paper and allied products, and 48.4 percent for automotive repair. These figures suggest that although industry was harmed by rising petroleum prices in the near term, the long-term effects of those price rises were mollified by substantial operating and production adjustments.

The analysis presented above demonstrates that industries that made the greatest reductions in petroleum inputs following the price hikes of 1973 and 1979 experienced the smallest declines in profitability. Certainly, the extent of a given industry's declining profit margin was partly determined by varying elasticities of demand. For example, firms that faced relatively inelastic demand for their products (e.g., drug companies) would simply pass the rising fuel costs on to consumers rather than burden themselves with reducing their demand for petroleum-derived products. Conversely, businesses that faced an elastic demand relationship (e.g., hotels and lodgings) risked reducing consumer demand if they raised prices, and so they needed to either cut petroleum inputs or absorb the increased costs themselves. Even taking into account the issue of elasticity, it was still the firm's relative success in implementing conservation measures and altering production procedures during periods of rising oil prices that most impacted profitability.

Industry Profits in the Oil-Dependent Sectors

The rates of return on sales for the industries with the highest utilization of petroleum are presented in Table 4.9 and Figure 4.1. All four sectors experienced significant declines in profitability in 1974 as a result of the oil price shock of the previous year: 31.1 percent in the home-building industry, 21.4 percent in the utilities sector, 11.0 percent in the retail trade, and 9.9 percent in the area of hotels and lodgings. These industries then experienced varying rates of recovery before the second oil shock of 1979. In home building, profits rebounded in 1975, but then began a long decline that was not strictly related to petroleum prices. For the utilities, profitability remained depressed for the remainder of the

Table 4.8

Petroleum Inputs for Selected Industries: Actual Figures Versus Projections Using 1972 Ratios, 1982

SIC Code	Sector	Projected	Actual	% Difference
02	Other Agriculture	61.7	12.05	−80.5
11	New Construction	19.1	4.02	−79.0
12	Maintenance/Repair Construction	53.3	7.05	−86.8
24	Paper/Allied Products	13.1	6.45	−50.8
65	Transportation and Warehousing	62.6	19.32	−69.1
68	Electric/Gas/Water Utilities	39.5	13.52	−65.8
69	Wholesale/Retail Trades	22.0	6.07	−72.4
75	Auto Repair Services	10.0	5.18	−48.4

Source: Figures are derived from Tables 4.4 and 4.6.

decade. In retailing, a sustained recovery was under way by 1975. In the hotel trade, profits did not fully recover until 1977. All four industries learned a valuable lesson from the sharp rise in oil prices in 1973: Reduce reliance on petroleum inputs or suffer the economic consequences. By adopting more energy-efficient processes and utilizing alternative fuels, these industries insulated themselves from the impact of the second oil price hike of 1979, averaging a meager drop of only 2.0 percent in their profits for 1980 (the hotel industry even managed to increase its earnings from 1979 to 1980). From 1981 to 1986, the homebuilding and retailing sectors saw mixed profit margins, the utilities experienced a sustained recovery, and the hotel trade began a long downward turn.

Industry Profits in Less Oil-Dependent Sectors

Table 4.10 presents the figures for six less energy-dependent sectors for the period from 1972 to 1986 (the pattern for the four most affected sectors is illustrated in Figure 4.2). As would be expected, these sectors were far less impacted by the vagaries of the oil market. In fact, while some of these industries experienced slight downturns in profits following the price hikes of the 1970s, others actually saw their rates of return rise. Thus the figures for 1974 show moderate declines in profits for the following industries: food products, down 10.7 percent; chemicals, 6.0 percent; and drugs and

Table 4.9

Industry Profit-Sales Ratios for Selected Energy-Intensive Sectors, 1972–1986

Year	Home-building	Utilities	Retail Trade	Hotels
1972	15.25	12.79	8.08	17.01
1973	15.39	12.36	8.52	16.32
1974	10.60	9.71	7.58	14.70
1975	12.10	9.68	8.49	14.47
1976	10.93	9.90	9.01	15.90
1977	9.41	9.71	9.60	17.36
1978	8.75	9.57	9.54	18.95
1979	9.74	9.29	9.62	19.16
1980	9.47	8.74	9.31	20.57
1981	6.57	8.94	9.44	20.36
1982	7.48	10.01	9.72	19.98
1983	8.46	11.37	10.42	16.64
1984	2.54	11.84	9.91	16.48
1985	5.33	12.04	9.13	16.49
1986	6.31	12.57	9.31	15.37

Source: Standard and Poor's Corporation, *Industry Surveys*. The figures for electric utilities represent earnings as a percentage of operating revenues.

Note: Home-building comprises figures for both new and maintenance construction.

cleansing preparations, 3.6 percent. But other sectors saw increased profits from 1973 to 1974: paper, up 12.0 percent; steel, 20.8 percent; and aluminum, 20.2 percent. The rate of return for paper was somewhat puzzling given the industry's higher dependence on petroleum inputs than the other sectors included in the table (in comparison, petroleum represented less than 1 percent of total inputs for the steel and aluminum sectors).

There is no discernible pattern in profit margins for the six sectors in the interim period between 1973–1974 and the second oil shock of 1979. In studying the rates of return from 1979 to 1980, increases were seen in the food, paper, and chemical sectors (with profits improving by 0.6 percent, 2.3 percent, and 13.2 percent, respectively), while decreases were experienced in the drug, steel, and aluminum industries (down 7.7 percent, 19.1 percent, and 3.2 percent, respectively). The decline in the steel industry is at least partly attributable to foreign competition and the resulting downward pressure on prices.

The figures presented in Tables 4.9 and 4.10 demonstrate that each industry reacted differently to the rising oil prices of the 1970s. Even in the case of sectors that relied heavily on petroleum inputs (e.g., the retail trade and the hotel business), conservation and substitution measures greatly offset the blow of inflated oil prices. Ultimately, it was the

Figure 4.1   **Industry Profit-Sales Ratios for Four Energy-Intensive Sectors, 1972–1986**

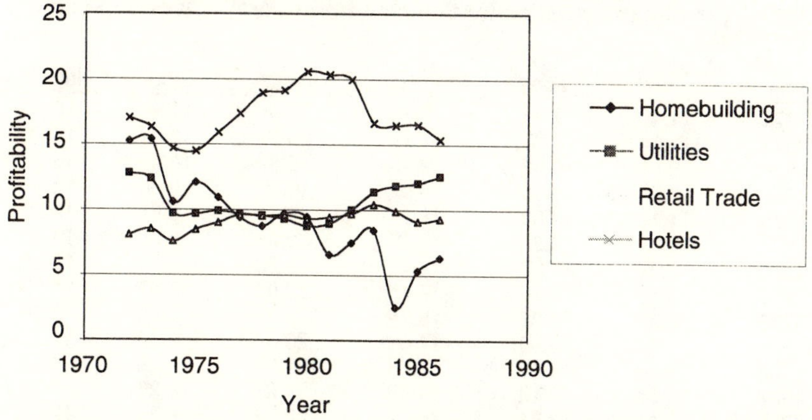

oil-dependent sectors with rigid input requirements—notably, the utilities—that proved to be least capable of adjusting their industry practices to the upturn in petroleum prices. The changes in industry profitability discussed above must now be placed in the larger context of cyclical variations in the gross domestic product.

Business Cycles and Industry Profitability

In considering the decline in profitability experienced by U.S. industry between 1972 and 1982, one must compare the relative impact of business cycle variations versus the effects of rising oil prices. During this period, there were three distinct downturns in domestic industrial production: between 1973 and 1975, when output fell 10.2 percent; from 1979 to 1980, when the drop was 2.8 percent; and in 1981 to 1982, when the Federal Reserve squeezed out inflation by devising a 5.3 reduction. Using the correlation coefficients for the industries analyzed in Tables 4.9 and 4.10, it becomes clear that, with few exceptions, it was not the declining output of these recessions but rather petroleum prices that exerted greater downward pressure on industry profits.

The correlation between profitability and petroleum prices in the electrical utilities sector was –0.47, a number that shows how greatly the industry's fortunes were suppressed by the rising cost of oil inputs. The effect of the business cycle on that sector's rate of return was also significant, with a correlation of 0.50. In the food and chemical sectors, the correlations between petroleum prices and profits were –0.55 and –0.79, respectively, but the correlations between industrial production and prof-

Table 4.10

Industry Profit-Sales Ratios for Selected Non-Energy-Intensive Sectors, 1972–1986

Year	Food	Paper	Chemicals	Drugs	Steel	Aluminum
1972	11.40	12.24	19.88	20.96	11.26	13.58
1973	11.04	14.67	21.16	20.63	12.04	13.76
1974	9.86	16.43	19.90	19.89	14.54	16.54
1975	10.72	15.50	18.97	19.62	10.30	12.17
1976	11.19	15.69	19.17	19.44	8.64	12.20
1977	9.38	14.87	18.15	20.21	5.59	13.98
1978	11.03	14.62	18.46	20.72	8.91	16.20
1979	9.45	13.70	17.47	20.84	7.97	16.69
1980	9.51	14.01	19.78	19.24	6.45	16.16
1981	10.04	10.80	14.68	20.04	7.83	11.15
1982	10.20	8.42	13.74	21.58	2.28	4.52
1983	10.54	10.72	14.48	22.23	4.23	7.75
1984	10.12	13.81	15.96	22.72	8.71	12.06
1985	10.74	13.64	16.03	23.55	8.68	9.18
1986	11.11	15.49	19.11	25.60	8.13	12.26

Source: Standard and Poor's Corporation, *Industry Surveys*.
Note: The aluminum industry was used as a surrogate for primary nonferrous metals.

Figure 4.2   **Industry Profit-Sales Ratios for Four Less Energy-Intensive Sectors**

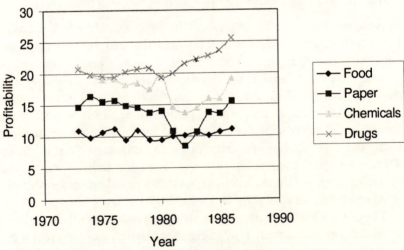

itability were insignificant. Owing to their ability to quickly adjust to rising petroleum prices, the retail, hotel, and pharmaceutical companies were less susceptible to cyclical downturns in production. Only certain sectors of U.S. industry (e.g., utilities, food, and chemicals) were harmed in the long run by the dual petroleum price shocks of the 1970s.

COMMODITY MARKET INSTABILITY AND
INFLATION AT THE CONSUMER LEVEL

The series of oil price hikes of the 1970s contributed more to the general rise in prices in the United States than any other factor. The most dramatic rise in inflation occurred in the markets for petroleum-derived products, notably gasoline and heating oil. The price of gasoline, which averaged $0.38 per gallon in 1972, rose to $0.55 per gallon by 1974. Table 4.11 illustrates the path of gasoline and fuel oil prices from 1972, through the second oil price shock in 1979, to the de facto collapse of OPEC in 1986. During this period, the CPI rose by just over 160 percent, while gasoline prices increased 171 percent. This parity suggests that the run-up in oil prices had pushed the consumer cost of gasoline up only slightly faster than the general rate of inflation. These relative price changes must be placed in the context of the general acceleration of inflation caused by OPEC's actions.

The direct link between rising fuel prices and the cost of essential consumer goods is discernible because of the minimal processing required to convert crude oil into products for final consumption. When OPEC oversaw the nearly 300 percent increase in the price of oil between 1972 and 1974, from $2.80 to $11.22 per barrel, the retail price of gasoline shot up to $0.31 per gallon, exclusive of tax (Table 4.11). Then when the cartel became quiescent between 1974 and 1978, petroleum prices increased by only 15.4 percent and consumer energy costs rose only modestly. The oil price shock of 1979 resulted in renewed energy inflation, and the price of gasoline rose by 110 percent between 1978 and 1981. During the same period, the retail cost of heating oil rose by 135 percent. As shown in Figure 4.3, rising energy prices contributed greatly to the overall elevation in the CPI during this period, with the largest increases seen in 1974 and 1979 through 1981.

After 1981, consumers benefited from gradually falling gasoline and heating oil prices. Between 1981 and 1986, the cost of gasoline fell by 29 percent and the average price at the pump stood at $0.56 (exclusive of tax). At the same time, consumers enjoyed a 30.7 percent drop in heating oil prices. The fact that consumer energy prices never declined to the same degree that wholesale petroleum prices fell is not surprising given the generalized inflation of the 1970s (the CPI rose 117 percent between 1972 and 1981).

Commodity Costs and Consumer Prices for Lightly
Processed Nonpetroleum Products

The link between commodity costs and specific consumer prices is strongest when the product undergoes only nominal processing before it is

Table 4.11

Index of Gasoline and Fuel Oil Prices in the United States, 1972–1988
(1982–1984 = 100)

Year	Gasoline	Heating Oil
1972	28.4	—
1973	31.2	—
1974	42.2	32.3
1975	45.1	35.0
1976	47.0	37.5
1977	49.7	43.0
1978	51.8	45.5
1979	70.2	74.5
1980	97.5	88.2
1981	108.5	106.9
1982	102.6	106.1
1983	99.4	96.5
1984	97.8	98.5
1985	98.6	94.6
1986	77.0	74.1
1987	80.1	75.8
1988	80.8	75.8

Source: U.S. Department of Labor, *Monthly Labor Review.*

Figure 4.3   **Petroleum Prices and the Cost of Gasoline and Heating Oil, 1972–1987**

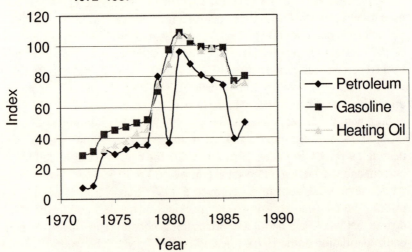

sold at the retail level. Thus, like petroleum, cocoa, coffee, and sugar also experience price movements that are parallel in nature. Coffee prices at the consumer level, for example, are largely determined by the costs of the beans themselves, with the roasting and grinding processes adding only minimally to the production outlays. A comparison of the spot price of Brazilian coffee beans to the price paid by consumers from 1972 to 1988 demonstrates how these costs move in tandem (Table 4.12). Indeed, the tripling of bean prices between 1974 and 1976 was accompanied by a similar jump in retail costs, and the rapid decline in the price of beans after 1980 resulted in a commensurate drop in consumer prices. The correlation coefficient between international and consumer prices for coffee for the period from 1974 to 1988 was 0.406. Even factoring in the rising costs of processing, transportation, and marketing during this period, the figure is still quite high. Consequently, consumers can anticipate that price changes in the wholesale coffee market will translate into equivalent changes in the prices that they face in the supermarket or at the local espresso bar.

Commodity Costs and Consumer Prices for Highly Processed Nonpetroleum Products

The price configuration in the bauxite, rubber, and tin markets is entirely different from nominally processed commodities, for these raw materials are but one of many inputs in manufacturing processes, and therefore the connection between the costs of the resources and the final prices paid by consumers is weak. Natural rubber, for example, is heavily processed before it assumes a form that can be used by consumers. Most of the world's natural rubber becomes the input for automobile tires, and the number of steps taken from the time that the raw material is harvested until it takes the form of a radial—with each stage of processing adding to the manufacturing, labor, and transportation costs—ensures that the connection between the price of the commodity and the cost of the final product will be weak. The price comparisons for natural and crude or processed rubber presented in Table 4.13 and Figure 4.4 demonstrate that even at this first stage of processing, the link between prices is already tenuous. Indeed, as natural rubber prices rose 144 percent between 1975 and their peak in 1980, processed rubber prices rose by only 81.5 percent. Similarly, when natural rubber prices fell 43 percent between 1980 and 1985, the cost of processed rubber actually rose by a little over 2 percent. The expense of processing crude rubber, which had been rising along with the CPI in the 1970s, had become dominant, and therefore the bond between natural and processed rubber prices became less apparent.

Table 4.12

Price of Commodity Coffee Beans and Coffee at the Consumer Level, 1972–1988 (in dollars per pound and as a price index [1982–1984 = 100])

Year	Beans: $	Consumer Price
1974	0.78	160.5
1975	0.82	172.9
1976	1.57	243.6
1977	2.42	451.2
1978	1.85	420.7
1979	1.83	101.8
1980	1.92	111.6
1981	1.28	96.2
1982	1.40	98.5
1983	1.32	98.8
1984	1.44	102.7
1985	1.45	105.5
1986	1.95	132.7
1987	1.12	116.2
1988	1.35	115.0

Source: International coffee prices are derived from figures presented in Table 3.1. Consumer prices for coffee are taken from the U.S. Department of Labor, *Monthly Labor Review-CPI Detail Report.*

By the final stage of production, when automobile tires come out of the factory, the link between rubber prices and consumer prices is even less discernible. The 144 percent rise in the price of natural rubber between 1975 and 1980 was accompanied by a 59.5 percent increase in tire prices. Not surprisingly, the increased price of tires was more closely related to the rising costs of processed rubber, the direct input of tire manufacturing. When natural rubber prices dropped rapidly (if erratically) between 1980 and 1985, declining 42.7 percent, tire prices were essentially flat (up an inconsequential 0.2 percent).

The connection between commodity prices and consumer costs is even weaker for tin. Tin's many attributes—its malleability, nontoxicity, and noncorrosiveness—make it a desirable component in many industries, notably those of commercial canning, soldering compounds, circuit boards, anticorrosive steel, dental amalgams, and chemical compounds. In 1997, 44,300 tons of tin were utilized by U.S. industries (just over 80 percent of this amount, 36,100 tons, was imported, with the remainder coming from reclaimed scrap tin). The solder industry consumed nearly 36 percent (15,900 tons) of the total supply, followed by the tin-plating and chemical sectors (with 21.0 percent and 18.4 percent of the aggregate, respectively). The

Table 4.13

Index of Natural Rubber and Processed Rubber Prices Versus the Producer Price of Tires, 1974–1988 (1977 = 100)

Year	Natural Rubber	Processed Rubber	Tires
1974	95.7	81.2	78.7
1975	71.9	84.8	87.6
1976	95.0	93.8	95.2
1977	100.0	100.0	100.0
1978	119.2	109.3	105.7
1979	156.5	128.9	121.4
1980	175.5	153.9	139.7
1981	138.5	164.1	147.8
1982	108.9	162.4	150.5
1983	134.6	163.5	144.7
1984	119.2	161.2	142.9
1985	100.5	157.5	140.0
1986	103.1	148.1	138.0
1987	121.4	155.0	137.0
1988	139.7	175.8	141.5

Source: U.S. Department of Commerce, *Statistical Abstract of the United States.*

Figure 4.4 **Natural and Crude Rubber Prices and the Price of Tires, 1974–1988**

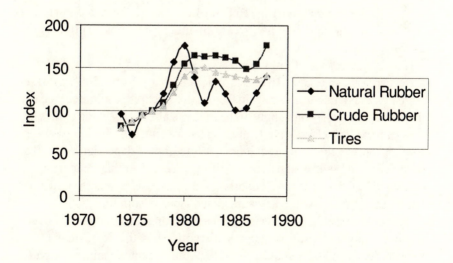

amount of tin needed in other manufacturing processes, however, is generally quite small and so the metal's cost is inconsequential to production expenditures. Indeed, the doubling of tin prices between 1974 and 1980 had virtually no impact on U.S. industry.

STRATEGIC STOCKPILES OF THE UNITED STATES

As detailed earlier in this chapter, the United States created the Strategic Petroleum Reserve after the oil price shock and embargo of 1973 in order to safeguard the economy from future supply disruptions. The other stockpiles maintained by the U.S. government are devoted to critical minerals, that is (with the exception of zinc), raw materials considered critical to domestic defense industries and national security. Table 4.14 provides a breakdown of these holdings in 1980 and 1994. The volume of these stocks can be illustrated by comparing the level of these reserves to the annual domestic utilization of each mineral.

In 1994, the United States imported 10.7 million metric tons of bauxite (the lowest figure since 1988), industry used 11.2 million metric tons, and an additional 129,000 metric tons were exported. These figures represent a deficit of 629,000 metric tons, and since there is no domestic mining of bauxite, the aluminum industry was forced to dip into its holdings to make up the difference. As illustrated in Table 4.14, U.S. strategic reserves of bauxite in 1994 totaled 16.5 million long tons (2,240 pounds each) or 16.8 million metric tons, a figure that represented one and one-half years of industrial consumption (U.S. Defense Logistics Agency).

The U.S. reserves of tin, which stood at 145,000 metric tons in 1994, were also large in relation to consumption. In that year, 42,200 tons of tin were utilized in manufacturing. In theory, the stockpile contained a nearly three-and-one-half-year supply of the mineral, although, owing to the success of recycling efforts, the United States was not wholly dependent on foreign sources for its tin requirements (the import dependence stood at 83 percent in 1994, which means that the reserves in that year were the equivalent of four years of imports). The size of U.S. reserves of both bauxite and tin far exceed any anticipated lapse in supply.

Although the cobalt, manganese, platinum, and tungsten markets have not been subject to serious supply disruptions in the past, their indispensability to industry requires that the United States maintain significant reserves. Of the 68,539 kilograms of platinum and related metals

Table 4.14

U.S. Stockpiles of Critical Materials, 1980 and 1994

Mineral	Units	Inventory, by Year	
		1980	1994
Bauxite	Million long tons	14.3	16.5
Tin	Thousand metric tons	200	145
Zinc	Thousand short tons	380	360
Cobalt	Million lbs.	41	52
Manganese	Thousand short tons	5,130	2,792
Tungsten	Million lbs.	97	82
Titanium	Thousand short tons	43	37
Platinum	Thousand Troy oz.	466	453

Source: U.S. Defense Logistics Agency.

Note: Minerals included are those regarded as essential for both military and industrial preparedness in times of national emergency.

utilized by U.S. industry in 1994, 62,370 kilograms was imported.[5] The domestic stockpile of 453,000 troy ounces or 14,119.5 kilograms of platinum is the equivalent of a two-and-one-half-months supply. The meagerness of these reserves can be attributed to two factors. First, although the automotive, chemical, computer, and electrical industries are highly dependent on platinum, its high cost—$438 per troy ounce as of December 1999—discourages the stockpiling of significant amounts of the metal. Secondly, Canada extracts nearly 8,300 kilograms of platinum each year, and therefore the United States has a secure source for its industry requirements.

In contrast to platinum stockpiles, reserves of tungsten represent many years of consumption (82 million pounds or 37.3 million kilograms in 1994). In that year, total requirements of tungsten were at unusually low levels, but if one considers the numbers over the period from 1992 to 1996, then the average annual consumption can be placed at 4,510 metric tons. Domestic reserves of tungsten were therefore equivalent to an eight-year supply. This level may appear excessive, but the indispensability of the material in the production of hardened steel makes it a critical input in the defense industry. In addition, because tungsten is relatively cheap ($52.6 per metric ton on the London market in 1996), it is economically feasible to maintain substantial stockpiles of the metal.

The U.S. stockpile of manganese stood at 2,792,000 short tons (1,269,100 metric tons) in 1994. As with tungsten, the critical role that manganese plays in producing hardened steel, including applications in defense manufacturing, explains the need for reserves of this size. The United States possesses no native deposits of manganese, so in 1996 alone, the country imported 478,000 metric tons of manganese ore, 374,000 tons of ferromanganese, and 323,000 tons of silicomanganese. Owing to the variations in manganese content in these three mineral compounds, it is difficult to determine the precise magnitude of U.S. reserves. Based on past import figures, it could be reasonably asserted that the 1.3–million-metric-ton stockpile held in 1994 represented about a one-year supply of the mineral.

Cobalt is yet another mineral critical to the production of steel alloys, particularly those utilized by the aerospace industry in producing jet engines. In 1994, the United States maintained a reserve of 52 million pounds (23,636 metric tons) of the metallic element. Since the country neither produces nor refines cobalt, it relies heavily on imports. In 1996, for example, 6,710 metric tons or 76 percent of inputs were imported, with the remaining 2,100 metric tons recovered domestically through recycling. Thus the U.S. stockpile represents 2.7 years of total consumption, but if one factors in the reclaimed material, this number rises to nearly three and one-half years. Domestic reserves of this critical substance have been increasing since 1987. The stockpiling has increased despite the rising cost of cobalt: $6.56 per pound in 1987, increasing nearly 300 percent to $25.50 per pound in 1996. In the latter year, U.S. holdings were worth over $1.3 billion on international commodity markets.

In contrast to some of the minerals discussed above, which are crucial to U.S. defense industries but are not produced domestically, zinc is a material not essential to military applications and for which indigenous deposits exist. Consequently, U.S. reserves of zinc are relatively small. The stockpile of slab zinc and zinc ore was 360,000 short tons or 327,300 metric tons in 1994. Like manganese, there is a wide range of purity in zinc ore, making it somewhat difficult to estimate the precise size of these reserves in relation to annual consumption. If one looks back to 1996, when the United States consumed approximately 1.45 million metric tons of slab zinc and zinc ore (mostly in the metal alloys industry), then the stockpile could be calculated as having represented approximately a three-month supply. The relative insignificance of U.S. holdings of zinc not only indicates the benign applications of the mineral but also reflects domestic self-sufficiency. In 1996, for example, imports comprised only 33 percent of annual consumption. Clearly, the

United States would have little difficulty coping with an interruption in the supply of zinc.

The maintenance of reserves of essential commodities provides a buffer against price instability in international markets. Although most of the minerals that are stockpiled are considered strategic materials, petroleum, tin, and zinc are held primarily for economic reasons. The existence of significant caches of key materials can counter the market manipulations of cartels, for rapid price increases can be tempered through the measured release of materials from these holdings. It is likely that the United States will continue to maintain significant stockpiles of crucial products as a means of ensuring economic stability.

SUBSTITUTION AS A RESPONSE TO RISING COMMODITY PRICES

The rapid increase in commodity prices seen in the 1970s provided many developing nations with an economic windfall. This was particularly true for the petroleum-exporting nations, which saw their export revenues quadruple between 1972 and 1973 while the quantity of oil being shipped remained fairly constant. By 1979, prices had risen an astonishing 1,400 percent over their levels of 1972. Inflation of prices in the other commodity markets was far less extreme, with rubber and tin prices up 100 percent and coffee prices up 150 percent between 1974 and 1980. From 1974 to 1977, cocoa experienced a price elevation of approximately 150 percent. Not surprisingly, at both the governmental and corporate levels, the industrialized nations began to turn toward more affordable alternatives or synthetic replacements for these commodities. This process of substitution resulted in a chorus of complaints from the developing nations, whose export earnings depended on a narrow range of raw materials.

The rubber market provides a perfect illustration of the pitfalls of single-commodity exporting vis-à-vis product substitution. As detailed in chapter 3, price increases have promoted substitution of synthetic rubber for natural rubber in many commercial applications. In fact, even though synthetic rubber is irreplaceable in certain products, notably the tire industry, fabricated rubber now accounts for a larger share of total world output than the raw material. Since these petroleum-derived synthetic products are exclusively manufactured in industrialized countries, it behooves the developing nations to exercise restraint in their manipulation of prices and supplies.

Table 4.15

U.S. Fossil Fuel Energy Consumption by Type, 1973–1985 (in quadrillions of BTUs)

Year	Petroleum	Natural Gas	Coal	Total
1973	34.8	22.5	13.0	70.3
1974	33.4	21.8	12.7	67.9
1975	32.7	20.0	12.6	65.3
1976	35.2	20.4	13.6	69.2
1977	37.2	19.9	13.	71.0
1978	38.0	20.0	13.7	71.7
1979	37.1	20.7	15.0	72.8
1980	34.2	20.4	15.4	70.0
1981	32.0	19.9	15.9	67.8
1982	30.2	18.5	15.3	64.0
1983	30.0	17.3	15.9	63.2
1984	31.0	18.5	17.0	66.5
1985	30.9	17.8	17.5	66.2

Source: U.S. Department of Commerce, *Statistical Abstract of the U.S.*

The U.S. response to the OPEC-driven oil price increases of the 1970s, which included the implementation of successful conservation measures, provides another instructive example of restructured commodity demand. Of the 70.3 quadrillion BTUs of fossil-fuel energy consumed by the domestic economy in 1973, 49.5 percent was in the form of oil, 32 percent came from natural gas, and 18.5 percent was derived from coal. As illustrated in Table 4.15, U.S. consumption of fossil fuel rose slightly after 1973, reached a peak in 1979, and then declined. By the time of the recession of 1981–1982, the total consumption of fossil fuels had fallen 10 percent from the levels of 1973. Although this use rebounded somewhat after 1983, the total number of BTUs consumed in 1985 remained below the figure for 1973. The fact that this energy usage dropped between 1973 and 1985, even as the economy underwent substantial expansion, indicates how effectively industry reduced consumption in the face of higher energy prices.

The mechanism by which U.S. industry reacted most forcefully to rising oil prices was the substitution of domestically abundant coal for petroleum (see Figure 4.5). Following the price shock of 1973, U.S. consumption of crude oil dropped 6 percent over two years and then increased slightly in the later 1970s as the economy expanded. By 1981, however, petroleum use had declined below the level of 1973, to 47.2 percent of carbon-based energy inputs. The relative importance of natu-

Figure 4.5   **U.S. Fossil Fuel Consumption in BTUs**

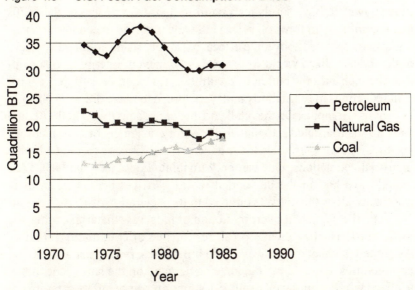

ral gas dropped even more rapidly, so that by 1985 it represented only 26.8 percent of fossil-fuel inputs. During this same period, however, coal usage was on the upswing, rising to 22 percent of the total BTUs of energy consumed by 1980. By 1985, coal made up over 26.4 percent of energy use; at this point, it had become as important as natural gas to the U.S. economy. Clearly, during the 1970s and early 1980s, the substitution of coal for petroleum was a modest but nonetheless significant factor in reducing OPEC's control over international prices.

CONCLUSION

However briefly, most of the cartels that formed in the 1970s managed to control the price of commodities. Yet although rising bauxite, cocoa, coffee, and rubber prices impacted specific U.S. industries, the effect on the economy as a whole was minor. In contrast, the dramatic rise in the price of petroleum produced significant and lasting effects in most sectors and resulted in the general stagnation of growth and accelerating inflation in the United States. The industrialized nations of Western Europe also experienced meaningful, if somewhat less dramatic, increases in unemployment and inflation due to rising oil prices. The recent resurgence of OPEC as a formidable economic force suggests that the developed nations will once again be subjected to inflationary pressures from disruptions in the oil market. The petroleum-exporting nations, however, have surely learned from their experiences of the 1970s and are unlikely to force oil prices to levels that lead to economic crisis.

As demonstrated above, the effects of rapidly rising commodity prices in the industrialized world were extremely uneven. Energy-intensive industries such as home building and utilities, for example, suffered significant reductions in profitability and were forced to make dramatic changes in their use of inputs. On the retail end, the cartel activity of the 1970s and early 1980s translated into higher prices for consumers of cocoa, coffee, and tires, which contributed to the general rise in prices experienced in the industrialized nations. One can only imagine the impact that UNCTAD would have had in the developed world if it had been successful in cartelizing all of the markets targeted in its declaration of 1976.

Given the persistent overproduction of most raw materials, it may be difficult to visualize a widespread resurgence of commodity inflation. As argued in chapter 5, however, the limited reserves of certain mineral commodities, coupled with increasing demand on the part of the industrialized world, could well result in a situation where inflation returns. It is in the interest of the developed countries to negotiate more favorable terms of trade with commodity exporters in exchange for price restraints in the future, but, to date, this approach has not been fruitful. If no accommodation can be reached, then nations that depend on commodity exports for their revenues may become restless and once again collude to raise prices.

NOTES

1. An interesting exception to this is the situation that developed with sugar, whose price peaked at $642 per metric ton in 1975. As argued in chapter 3, sugar is different from other commodities because its production is widely dispersed among both developing and developed nations. Consequently, the sugar price hike of the mid-1970s was an aberration and the market was left essentially untouched by the persistent commodity price inflation of the period.

2. Although it might be expected that increased growth in the money supply would result in higher-than-anticipated growth, ultimately, the outcome is an acceleration in inflation. Thus, although Hickman's work suggested that the Federal Reserve's policy may have lessened the impact of the oil price shocks on real GDP, in fact, it actually contributed to the higher inflation of the 1970s.

3. It has to be kept in mind that the prices of coal and natural gas, energy sources indigenous to the United States, also rose significantly after the OPEC price shock of 1973. The incentive of industry to substitute these energy inputs for petroleum was therefore lessened.

4. The analysis presented here has been confined to those years in which input-output coefficients were calculated for the U.S. economy. One must be cautioned that the instability of the coefficients over time could bias results derived from the figures.

5. The U.S. Geological Survey groups platinum, palladium, iridium, osmium, rhodium, and ruthenium together in the category of "Platinum and Allied Metals." The relative importance of each to domestic manufacturing was utilized to determine the demand for platinum only.

REFERENCES

Alm, A., and Weiner, R., eds. 1984. *Oil Shock: Policy Response and Implementation*. Cambridge, MA: Ballinger.

Bohi, D. 1989. *Energy Price Shocks and Macroeconomic Performance*. Washington, DC: Resources for the Future.

Darby, M. 1982. "The Price of Oil and World Inflation and Recession." *American Economic Review* 72, no. 4: 738–751.

Energy Modeling Forum. 1991. *International Oil Supply and Demand*. Stanford: Energy Modeling Forum.

Fried, E., and Schultze, C. 1975. "Overview." In *Higher Oil Prices and the World Economy*, ed. E. Fried and C. Schultze, pp. 1–70. Washington, DC: Brookings Institution.

Hickman, B.; Huntington, H.; and Sweeney, J. 1987. *Macroeconomic Impacts of Energy Shocks*. Amsterdam: North-Holland Press.

Pindyck, R., and Rotemberg, J. 1984. "Energy Shocks and the Macroeconomy." In *Oil Shock*, ed. Alm and Weiner, pp. 97–120.

Plummer, J. 1984. "Institutional Alternatives for Financing and Operating the Strategic Petroleum Reserve." In *Oil Shock*, ed. Alm and Weiner, pp. 167–186.

Sweetnam, G. 1982. "Stockpile Policies for Coping with Oil-Supply Disruptions." In *Policies for Coping with Oil-Supply Disruptions*, ed. G. Horwich and E. Mitchell, pp. 82–98. Washington, DC: American Enterprise Institute.

U.S. Department of Energy. 1986. *International Energy Annual Outlook*. Washington, DC: U.S. Government Printing Office.

Verleger, P. 1994. *Adjusting to Volatile Energy Prices*. Washington, DC: Institute for International Economics.

5

Addressing the Problem of Commodity Price Instability

The failure of cartels to solve the problem of commodity price instability indicates that some other means must be found to manage the markets for key raw materials. Although futures markets provide a significant degree of price certainty, the 1970s demonstrated that prices can still become fundamentally unstable during periods of high and variable inflation rates. Despite UNCTAD's concerted efforts to promote collusive arrangements, the organization's effectiveness was undermined by the economic forces working against the cartelization process. It is in the interests of both developing and developed nations to work toward creating mechanisms that will stabilize the world's commodity markets.

As has been shown, the demise of most cartels was brought about by persistent overproduction that made achieving a target price impossible. In the future, however, the supply of many cartelized products—notably bauxite, petroleum, and tin—may be constrained by the limits of the world's known reserves. Even when additional deposits of these and other exhaustible resources are discovered, they may be of inferior quality and they will certainly be more expensive to exploit. It is likely that another round of commodity price inflation will take place sometime in the next century, but one hopes that it will be more controlled than the erratic market climate that prevailed in the 1970s.

The situation with depletable commodities is entirely different from that of renewable resources. Although there has been some success in introducing tropical products into new geographic areas (e.g., the development of the rubber industry in Malaysia through the planting of nonindigenous rubber trees), climatic requirements continue to limit the cultivation of cocoa, coffee, rubber, and sugar. As the standard of living in the developing world rises and world population grows, the consumption of these renewable commodities will increase and the current output of fields and forests will no longer be able to meet demand.

The chapter begins with an analysis of the concentration of nonrenewable resources and the anticipated years to depletion. Economic growth in the developed world would be expected to strain these resources further, and therefore a commodity demand crunch may occur even sooner than expected.

The second section of the chapter explores alternatives to cartels for the stabilization of world commodity markets. Among the government-sponsored initiatives, one must single out the European Union's STABEX system, which has provided subsidies to commodity producers in the developing world for over twenty-five years. Programs run by nongovernmental organizations (NGOs) will also be considered. The promising features of regional planning will be addressed, as will producer cooperatives. The chapter concludes with a discussion of commodity clearinghouses, whose history should serve as a cautionary lesson on the excesses of market manipulation.

WORLD RESERVES OF NONRENEWABLE RESOURCES: THEIR CONCENTRATION AND YEARS TO DEPLETION

A discussion of the concentration and lifetime of world reserves of nonrenewable resources should begin with an examination of the cartelized products of petroleum, bauxite, and tin. The likelihood of renewed commodity price inflation is greatest for energy reserves, particularly petroleum, the substantial sources of which are limited when compared to gas and coal. As the known deposits scattered in countries throughout the world become depleted, petroleum production will be even more concentrated than it is now.

Petroleum Reserves

In 1993, the world's reserves of recoverable petroleum stood at 140,676 million metric tons (Table 5.1 and Figure 5.1). Just over 67 percent of this amount was located in North Africa and the Middle East. The countries with the greatest percentages of these

Table 5.1

World Petroleum Reserves by Region, 1993
(in millions of metric tons and as a percentage of world output)

Nation/Region	Reserves	(%)
Algeria	1,183	0.84
Libya	5,931	4.22
Iran	12,700	9.02
Iraq	13,417	9.54
Kuwait	13,358	9.50
Saudi Arabia	35,620	25.32
United Arab Emirates	12,330	8.76
Total for Region	94,531	67.20
Venezuela	9,842	7.00
Mexico	6,906	4.91
United States	3,900	2.77
Russian Federation	6,670	4.74

Source: World Energy Council.

Figure 5.1   **Petroleum Reserves of Key Producers, 1993**

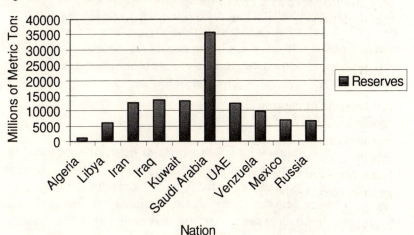

global petroleum holdings were Saudi Arabia, with 25.3 percent; Iraq, with 9.54 percent; Kuwait, with 9.50 percent; Iran, with 9.02 percent; and the United Arab Emirates, with 8.76 percent. This high concentration of reserves, together with the failure of the industrialized world to develop suitable petroleum substitutes, helped revitalize OPEC in 1999.

Bauxite Reserves

According to U.S. Geological Service estimates, the exploitable reserves of bauxite totaled 25,000 million metric tons in 1997. With world production of bauxite totaling 109,000 metric tons in 1997, the known reserves are therefore the equivalent of a 229-year supply. Alumina can be derived from other sources (e.g., corundum), but production costs would rise. The high concentration of bauxite suggests that exporting nations may have the ability to raise prices substantially in the future.

Tin Reserves

The world's tin resources are widely scattered throughout Asia and Latin America, with nine nations possessing proven reserves in excess of 200,000 metric tons (Table 5.2 and Figure 5.2). If extraction were to continue at the pace set in 1997, three of the major producers would have depleted their known reserves before the year 2025, and by 2047, all but four of the exporting nations would be eliminated as major sources of tin ore.[1] Should no new major deposits be discovered, then the dwindling number of producing nations could force prices up. But this inflation could result in substitution of less appropriate materials in the industries of canning, electrical components, transportation, and fabricated metals. In addition, aggressive efforts to recycle tin are likely to continue, further offsetting the power of the Tin Association.

Reserves of Other Critical Materials

Looking beyond the now familiar markets of petroleum, bauxite, and tin, one sees that attempts to cartelize the supply of nonrenewable materials have been largely unsuccessful. This failure is due not only to political differences between the producing nations, but also to the fact that many of the countries with reserves have laws forbidding collusive agreements.

The output of most of these raw materials is highly concentrated. The mining of chromium, for example, a critical input to the metallurgical and chemical industries, is centered in just three nations: India, Kazakhstan, and South Africa. Ninety percent of the production of cobalt, a key component in the manufacture of jet engines and chemical products, is concentrated in just six nations: Canada, Finland, Norway,

Table 5.2

Proven Reserves and Production of Tin, 1997 (in metric tons)

Country	Reserves[a]	Production	Years Remaining at Current Production Levels
Australia	210,000	10,000	21
Bolivia	450,000	15,000	30
Brazil	1,200,000	19,000	63
China	2,100,000	65,000	32
Indonesia	750,000	47,000	16
Malaysia	1,200,000	5,000	240
Peru	300,000	28,000	11
Russia	940,000	8,000	118
Thailand	180,000	1,000	180
World[b]	7,700,000	211,000	36

Source: U.S. Geological Service.
[a]The U.S. Geological Service provides two estimates of total reserves, the more conservative of which has been utilized here. The more liberal projection would raise the expected lifetime of world deposits to 57 years.
[b]This includes reserves and production from smaller producers such as Portugal.

Russia, Congo, and Zambia. The output of platinum, an indispensable input in many industries from the automotive to the electronic sectors, is mined largely in just two locales: South Africa and the former Soviet Union. Seventy-five percent of the world's known reserves of manganese, an essential input in the production of iron and steel, are also located in South Africa and the nations of the former Soviet Union. Titanium, used in the manufacture of both commercial and military jet engines, is produced by only a few nations, including China, Japan, Kazakhstan, Russia, and the United States. Conversely, zinc, used in only a limited capacity in industry (e.g., in the manufacture of rust-resistant steel), is produced by nearly fifty countries, including Australia, Canada, China, Mexico, Peru, and the United States. Finally, copper—a material with wide applications in the construction, electrical, machinery, and transportation equipment industries—is produced by many countries, including Australia, Canada, Chile, China, Indonesia, Mexico, Peru, Poland, Russia, the United States, and Zambia.

Keeping in mind the relative concentration of production of five of these seven key industrial commodities, one can now look to Table 5.3, which provides a list of corresponding reserves and estimates of the

Figure 5.2   **Tin Reserves of Key Producers, 1997**

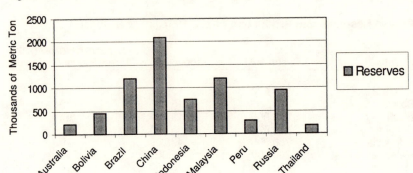

number of years that the known deposits will last under current levels of output. It would appear that the reserves of chromium, cobalt, platinum, and titanium—whose supplies are expected to last, variously, from three hundred to about one thousand years—would be so abundant as to discourage any form of cartelization. Moreover, despite the high concentration of production for each of these materials, a number of the suppliers are in the industrialized world and thus barred from even negotiating on prices. Indeed, of the four markets mentioned above, only those of chromium and platinum could conceivably be cartelized in the future. The possibility of cartelization of the copper and zinc markets is even more remote. Although their reserves are expected to last less than a century (only fifty-seven and eighty-three years, respectively), the fact that these materials are produced so widely and in several countries of the industrialized world suggests that there is little possibility of market cooperation. Of this group of materials, only manganese, with its high concentration of production and relatively short expected time to depletion, would seem to be a good candidate for cartelization.

ECONOMIC GROWTH AND COMMODITY IMPORTS

The figures presented above suggest that, with few exceptions, the proven reserves of critical minerals are sufficient to meet the needs of the industrialized nations well into the future. This assessment, however, is based on production levels for 1996. Therefore, if the consumption of these critical raw materials rises rapidly with economic growth, it is conceivable that the available supplies may become strained much ear-

Table 5.3

Proven Reserves of Critical Minerals, 1997 (in millions of metric tons)

Mineral	Reserves	Production	Years Remaining Using 1996 Production Levels
Chromium	7,500.0	12.20	615
Cobalt	9.0	0.03	300
Manganese	680.0	7.40	92
Platinum	0.7	0.15	450
Titanium	600.0	0.42	>1,000
Zinc	330.0	3.99	83
Copper	630.0	11.00	57

Note: Platinum is in thousands of metric tons.

lier than currently anticipated. The same situation could occur for certain renewable resources such as cocoa, coffee, and rubber, which are grown in regions now undergoing rapid economic development. At the same time that the cultivated land in these countries is claimed for housing, business, and infrastructure, worldwide preservation efforts are discouraging the clearing of tropical forests for new plantations. In addition, there has been a general rise in domestic consumption of the crops grown in these regions. Thus if world population and economic expansion continue at current levels, production of these commodities may eventually be insufficient to meet world demand.

The Link Between Growth and Commodity Demand

The potential for a resource crunch is likely only if there is a link between economic growth and demand for commodities. Table 5.4 and Figures 5.3 through 5.5 present data for U.S. industrial production from 1974 to 1996 and chart the relationship between GDP and the demand for bauxite, petroleum, and tin.[2] In the case of tin, there is no clear connection between industrial production and import demand. Despite a 70 percent rise in output between 1974 and 1996 and a radical drop in prices in 1986, U.S. imports of tin remained flat. Thus, although the proven reserves of tin are small in relation to yearly demand, it is unlikely that significant pressure on prices will develop in the near future.

It is difficult to ascertain a trend in the import demand for bauxite. The importation of 14,976,000 metric tons in 1974 was matched in only one ensuing year, 1980. By 1986, demand had fallen by 56.9 percent and a complete recovery never occurred. Presently, imports seem to have stabilized at just over 10 million tons. The weakened demand for bauxite can be attributed to increased aluminum recycling by consumers as well as the substitution of alternative materials (e.g., specialty steel) in the construction and automobile industries. As with tin, industrial growth simply has not resulted in greater demand for bauxite.

Not surprisingly, the situation that prevails for petroleum is quite different. As indicated in Table 5.4 and Figure 5.5, petroleum imports are closely correlated with industrial output. In fact, while U.S. industrial production rose just 70 percent between 1974 and 1996, demand for petroleum from foreign sources rose 116 percent. Although the elevation in import demand is partly explained by falling domestic production, demand for crude oil has, without question, risen along with U.S. growth. A simple correlation analysis that controls for prices suggests that a one percentage point rise in the index of industrial production results in an increase in petroleum imports of approximately 52,000 barrels per day. Consequently, future economic growth is likely to result in significant upward pressure on petroleum prices. This helps to explain OPEC's ability to reassert control over petroleum prices in 1999 (the price went from $12.00 per barrel in April to nearly $25.00 per barrel in September). All evidence indicates that oil prices will be impacted by cartel activity well into the future.

Growth and Demand for Consumer Products

The demand for consumer items such as coffee, cocoa, and rubber (for tires) is more likely to be influenced by growth in aggregate demand (real GDP) as opposed to industrial production. Table 5.5 presents figures for imports of these products versus growth in total output for the period from 1974 to 1996. The figures suggest that the levels of both cocoa and rubber imports are linked to changes in gross domestic product. Conversely, in spite of a near doubling of real GDP, coffee demand during this period changed little. The estimation of correlation coefficients for cocoa and rubber demonstrate the strong link between growth and import demand. Controlling for prices, a $1 billion rise in GDP results in the importation of an additional 38 metric tons of cocoa and an added 112 metric tons of rubber.[3] Although these figures appear to be quite small, they demonstrate that continued growth will lead to ever-increasing pressure on available supplies in the future.

Table 5.4

Index of U.S. Industrial Production (1990 = 100) **and Demand for Tin, Bauxite, and Petroleum, 1974–1996** (in thousands of metric tons for tin and bauxite; in millions of barrels for petroleum)

Year	Index	Tin	Bauxite	Petroleum
1974	70.3	39.6	14,976	1269.2
1975	64.1	43.7	11,529	1,498.2
1976	70.0	45.1	12,548	1,935.0
1977	75.7	47.8	12,989	2,397.5
1978	80.2	46.8	13,847	2,319.8
1979	82.8	48.4	13,780	2,379.4
1980	80.5	44.5	14,087	1,921.0
1981	81.9	41.9	12,802	1,604.5
1982	77.5	31.5	10,122	1,273.1
1983	80.4	33.2	7,601	1,215.1
1984	87.5	36.6	9,435	1,250.5
1985	89.0	35.8	7,158	1,168.4
1986	90.0	32.2	6,456	1,525.0
1987	94.2	32.7	9,156	1,706.0
1988	98.4	35.6	9,944	1,864.1
1989	100.2	35.8	10,893	2,132.7
1990	100.0	32.1	12,144	2,141.5
1991	98.0	33.2	11,871	2,143.3
1992	101.1	36.1	10,939	2,216.6
1993	104.6	39.1	11,621	2,477.3
1994	110.3	35.0	10,700	2,578.0
1995	115.7	38.6	10,100	2,639.0
1996	119.8	37.1	10,200	2,740.4

Source: Figures on industrial production are drawn from IMF, *International Financial Statistics*; demand figures are taken from CRB, *Commodity Yearbook*.

Figure 5.3   **U.S. Demand for Tin Versus Industrial Production**

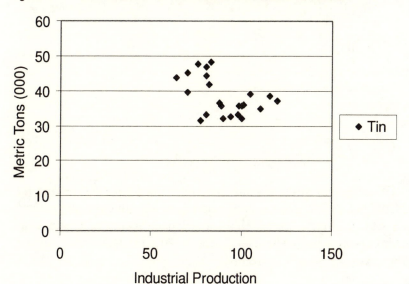

Figure 5.4   **U.S. Demand for Bauxite Versus Industrial Production**

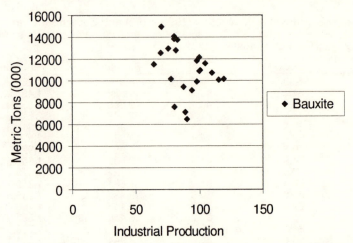

Figure 5.5   **U.S. Demand for Petroleum Versus Industrial Production**

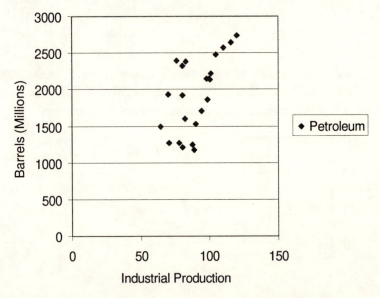

The remainder of this chapter discusses both cooperative and unilateral methods for raising commodity prices to benefit exporting nations. Given the likelihood that cartelization will once again affect major commodity markets, the industrialized nations should consider pursuing joint programs for market stabilization.

Table 5.5

**U.S. Economic Growth and Demand for Renewable Commodities,
1974–1996** (in 60-kg. bags for coffee and in thousands of metric tons for
cocoa and rubber)

Year	GDP	Coffee	Cocoa	Rubber
1974	3,891.2	19,245	230	681.3
1975	3,873.9	20,289	208	656.6
1976	4,082.9	19,788	225	712.9
1977	4,273.6	14,808	184	792.4
1978	4,503.0	18,133	163	746.2
1979	4,630.6	19,396	160	747.7
1980	4,615.0	18,153	142	585.0
1981	4,720.7	16,555	190	635.0
1982	4,620.3	17,416	199	585.0
1983	4,803.7	16,449	194	665.0
1984	5,140.1	17,734	209	750.7
1985	5,323.5	18,698	205	764.0
1986	5,487.7	19,483	200	743.0
1987	5,649.5	19,906	228	789.0
1988	5,865.2	15,348	241	858.3
1989	6,062.0	19,377	237	866.9
1990	6,136.3	19,566	270	807.5
1991	6,079.4	18,849	272	755.8
1992	6,244.4	21,673	307	910.2
1993	6,389.6	18,023	326	966.7
1994	6,610.7	14,913	317	1,001.7
1995	6,742.1	15,886	331	1,003.9
1996	6,928.4	17,947	345	1,001.7

Source: Figures for GDP are taken from *The Economic Report of the President,
1998.* Figures for coffee, cocoa, and rubber imports are taken from CRB, *Commodity
Yearbook.*

DESIGNING A CARTEL THAT WORKS: THE PROPER
MANAGEMENT OF BUFFER STOCKS

Rather than rely on "good faith" mechanisms like export controls and production limits to constrain supply, cartels should focus their energies on creating and utilizing buffer stocks. In the case of agricultural commodities, the
vagaries of weather may make it impossible for producing nations to exert
control over the ultimate level of output. A carefully managed buffer stock,
however, of the sort used by the International Tin Association prior to 1985,
can successfully control supply and achieve target prices.

The ultimate goal of a cartel is presumably the maximization of the
joint profits of the members through the regulation of prices. What is

frequently ignored in analyzing cartel behavior is the cost of the buffer stock, which in the case of some commodities has been substantial. In the absence of a collusive agreement, the aggregate profits of all exporters would be:

$$P(Q_T) \times Q_T - C(Q_T) \tag{1}$$

Where: $P(Q_T)$=World price of the commodity $(dP(Q_T)/dQ_T < 0)$
Q_T = Total world production
$C(Q_T)$ = Total cost incurred in producer $Q_T (dC(Q_T)/dQ_T > 0)$

The formation of a cartel effects both the price received by exporters as well as the costs incurred by each producer. For the cartel membership as a whole, the profits are:

$$\{P(Q_T - Q_s) \times (Q_T) - C(Q_T) - C_s(Q_s) \tag{2}$$
Where: $Q_T - Q_s$ = World supply after buffer stock purchases
$C_s(Q_s)$ = Cost of maintaining buffer stock

Equation (2) assumes that the cost of withdrawing commodities from the market to increase prices will rise as the size of the stockpile increases. Note that the quantity sold remains fixed at Q_T, as what is not sold on the world market has ultimately been purchased by the buffer stock.

Equation (2) illustrates, once again, how exporters of agricultural commodities face circumstances that are fundamentally different from those encountered by producers of minerals. In the international markets for cocoa, coffee, and sugar, Q_T is largely beyond the control of the cartel membership. As a consequence, Q_s will also be outside the cartel's domain, for this quantity is predetermined once Q_T and the target price are established. Conversely, nations that export tin, bauxite, and petroleum can control Q_T simply by accelerating or slowing production. If the target price and Q_T are set so that Q_s is zero, the costs associated with retaining a buffer stock are eliminated.

The first-order conditions for equation (2) are:

$$\frac{dp(Q_T - Q_S)}{dQ_T} \times Q_T + P(Q_T - Q_S) - C'(Q_T) = 0 \tag{3}$$

$$\frac{dP(Q_T - Q_S)}{dQ_S} \times Q_T - C_S'(Q_S) = 0 \qquad (4)$$

Equation (1) is the standard expression of profit maximization for any firm facing a downsloping demand curve. The marginal revenue associated with the last unit is equated to its marginal cost. Equation (4) equates the marginal cost of stockpiling the product to the increased revenue derived from restricting the supply of the product internationally.

Clearly, Q_T and Q_s are functionally linked. The greater the total output of cartel members, the greater the level of holdings required to maintain the established target price. For producers of agricultural commodities, Q_T remains largely beyond their control and it becomes imperative for exporters to select Q_s in order to maximize profits. For mineral producers, the choice of Q_T automatically results in a known level of Q_s, which is, ideally, zero.

COMMODITY PRICE STABILIZATION
WITHOUT CARTELS

STABEX: The European Union's Approach to
Balancing the Terms of Trade

Perhaps the most ambitious noncartel experiment undertaken in recent years to offset the negative effects of diminished export earnings is the program known as STABEX, which is financed under the European Development Fund. Initiated in 1975 under the first Lomé Convention, STABEX was conceived as a cooperative arrangement between the nations of the European Economic Community (now the European Union) and forty-six developing countries of Africa, the Caribbean, and the Pacific Rim (the so-called ACP nations).[4] Not coincidentally, many of the nations covered by the program were former colonies or territories of EU members. Under the original provisions of STABEX, disbursements were made to the ACP nations if their exports from mainly agricultural commodities traded below reference level earnings derived from average export revenues over several preceding years. In all but a few cases, only products exported to the EU or to other ACP countries—and goods not in competition with those from temperate regions—were eligible. The objective was to compensate producers for the revenues that would have been realized if market conditions had been stable (i.e., not af-fected by falling world prices, natural disasters, or a combination of the two). Allocations were made for a period of five years. Interference in the free play of markets was to be avoided. Rather, beneficiary countries were granted sole responsibility for how the funds were used. Transfers to most countries were made in the form of non-interest-bearing loans, which were to be repaid when commodity prices recovered or, in any event, by the end of the five-year reconstitution period. The least-developed ACP nations were granted transfers in the form of outright grants. In practice, however, all of the ACP nations came to treat the transfers like grants, and the EU, in turn, made little effort to secure repayment. Still in op-eration after twenty-five years (and three subsequent conventions, the first two devised on the same five-year schedule as Lomé I, the latest intended for the period from 1990 to 1994 but still in effect), STABEX has provided a flexible and constant source of subsidies to commodity exporters in the developing world.

The range of commodity markets that have enjoyed the protection of STABEX is remarkable (see Hewitt 1983, 1008–1009). So inclusive has the program been that even some producers of cocoa, coffee, and rubber were granted subsidies in the 1970s, at the same time that they were convening to form cartels. In addition to the staple commodities, STABEX expanded its program to include seafood, spices, seeds, and beans—products that had never before been the subject of market inter-vention. To place some limits on product claims, however, nations have been permitted to submit subsidy requests only for goods that represent a certain percentage of exports to all destinations. But here, a two-tier system has been followed, with the most impoverished nations (the so-called "Least Developed Landlocked and Island States" or LLIs) re-ceiving a lower export quotient. Under Lomé I, these export dependence thresholds were 7.5 percent and 2.5 percent, respectively.

The transfers issued under Lomé I were approximately $400 million (325 million ECU), with most of the disbursements made to African nations. The annual funding was, in fact, quite small in relation to the volume of trade over the five-year time frame of this phase of the pro-gram (the modest level of transfers has been a constant feature of the STABEX program). Nonetheless, a significant precedent was set when two-thirds of the total funding was dispersed as grants to LLIs. Of this amount, Senegal, Sudan, and Mauritania received one-half, this to sub-sidize the dip in the prices of groundnuts. In addition, only less than 5 percent of the recoverable loans issued to the other ACP nations was ever repaid. Hewitt argued that despite the abuses of the program, STABEX worked fairly smoothly in the 1970s, with payments matching the financial resources of the fund. The author noted, however, that the second round of STABEX, inaugurated by the Lomé II Convention of 1980, was on weaker financial footing, for steep declines in cocoa and coffee prices put the fund in the red. In fact, the program was able to dispense only just over 40 percent of subsidies promised in the statement for 1981–1982.

Under the Lomé II, Lomé III, and Lomé IV conventions (the latter two held in 1985 and 1990, respectively), the STABEX program expanded its coverage in terms of both the nations involved and the breadth of products eligible for subsidies. Negotiations under these later conventions reduced the export requirements for product inclusion. Under Lomé II, it was decided that the ACP nations with larger economies could apply for subsidies for commodities that comprised 6.5 percent of foreign sales; for the LLIs, the export percentage was set at only 2 percent. Under Lomé III, these two numbers were lowered to 6.0 percent and 1.5 percent, and under Lomé IV, they dropped even further, to 5.0 percent and 1 percent. The number of exports eligible for transfers has risen from the original twenty-six products to forty-four under Lomé II and fifty under Lomé IV. Concomitantly, the number of countries seeking payments has also grown, further stretching the program's resources.

The most sweeping changes to STABEX occurred in 1990, when under the provisions of Lomé IV, the direct, undifferentiated transfers granted to ACP nations since 1975 came to an end. In particular, the constant if unenforced principle that some beneficiary countries be required to reconstitute STABEX resources ceased, and transfers granted to all ACP countries were henceforth treated as nonrefundable grants. Resignedly, EU officials had been forced to address the fact that even by their own estimates, less than 10 percent of the overall resources of STABEX between 1975 and 1988 had been derived from reconstitution. Despite this apparent new liberality in funding, however, the monitoring of the allocations under Lomé IV was tightened considerably through the implementation of a "framework of mutual obligations" whereby the grants were negotiated between the recipient state and the commission on a case-by-case basis. The monies allocated for this phase of STABEX ($2.3 billion or 1.5 billion ECU) were targeted directly for the restructuring of those sectors experiencing the greatest drop in export earnings, and the payments were to be made in installments conforming to the various stages of projects undertaken. As might be expected, some of the ACP nations bristled at the tighter restrictions on the use of funds, but the EU has argued that with Lomé IV, a more long-term approach to the task of restructuring export activities and improving underlying conditions of production in the developing world was begun.

The goal of STABEX has been to compensate for downward movements in prices—to serve as a kind of insurance policy against lean years—rather than to establish stable markets. It is, therefore, short-sighted when compared to the buffer stock approach, which seeks long-term price certainty.

The history of STABEX in the 1990s under Lomé IV illustrates the unpredictability of the system in the face of changing commodity markets. Specifically, falling cocoa and coffee prices resulted in an obligation of $1.85 billion (1.38 billion ECU) in 1991. The resources of STABEX for that year, however, amounted to only $515 million (384 million ECU), which included $100.7 million (75 million ECU) "borrowed" from 1992 funding. The ACP-EEC Committee of Ambassadors negotiated the addition of $134 million (100 million ECU) to the fund, which resulted in $649.7 million (484 million ECU) in transfers (just over 35 percent of obligations). Coffee prices remained depressed in 1992 and so another $1.40 billion (1.06 billion ECU) was made in obligations, this despite the fact that STABEX resources amounted to only $473.9 million (391.5 million ECU) or approximately 38 percent of total requirements. Had this pattern of commodity prices continued, the STABEX system might have been crushed by the magnitude of funding requests. In 1993, in fact, negotiations on the level of funding broke down when the ACP nations refused to accept the EU's final offer for transfers.

To the relief of those involved in STABEX negotiations, commodity prices soared in 1994, resulting in a precipitous drop in obligations. Payments amounted to only $169.7 million (138 million ECU), far less than the $247.5 million (201.2 million ECU) allocated for that year. The most significant changes occurred in the coffee and cocoa markets, where prices rose significantly. As a result, the bulk of STABEX funding was transferred to the banana and cotton markets (which received 42.6 percent and 21.4 percent of obligations, respectively).

The persistent funding shortfalls of the STABEX system are partly due to the surprisingly wide array of products covered in the program. With the implementation of Lomé IV, approximately fifty product categories are now protected (versus twenty-six at the inception of STABEX). With these additions, items such as squid, shrimp, mangoes, beans, and lentils are now granted subsidies. This expansion of coverage not only increases the EU's obligation to the ACP nations already receiving STABEX funding, but it further increases the number of countries eligible for monies. As the product coverage continues to increase, it is likely that STABEX will again experience difficulties in funding its obligations.

STABEX and the Continued Overproduction of Commodities: A Need for Diversification

Clearly, the presence of too many products in any commodity market produces instability, and yet STABEX funding has seldom been directly targeted at diversifying the export mix of the ACP nations. Under Lomé IV, substantial allotments were granted to countries that faced declining coffee prices, and large allocations were directed to Caribbean nations for the restructuring of their struggling banana sectors. Very little, however, was done to channel money toward the development of new industries or the improvement of existing ones that would bring in fresh sources of revenue. Thus, although farmers' incomes and the overall quality of life in these regions have improved, the benefits realized by the beneficiary nations are actually quite short-lived, for while the subsidizations improve the productivity of the coffee fields and the banana plantations, increased yields contribute further to a worldwide surplus and falling prices. Had these funds been earmarked for the development of new tropical products that are high in demand, then the cycle of falling prices and increased production would have been broken. The history of STABEX funding under Lomé IV suggests that the EU will have to either increase contributions in the future or make a concerted attempt to promote product diversification.

In the few cases in which STABEX transfers were used for diversifying the exports of ACP nations, the allotments were made only after the needs of the country's "primary" markets were met. Thus, when Mauritania was granted monies to support the expansion of its mango sector, it was only after the country's fishing industry had been heavily subsidized. Similarly, Dominica first received funding to help offset the damage done to its banana sector by Hurricane Debbie, and only afterward were transfers made for the purpose of reducing the nation's dependence on this commodity. Finally, STABEX allocations for the improvement of the infrastructure of Vanuatu were distributed only after the declining profits from the island's market for coconut meat (copra) triggered funding. Like all transfers made under STABEX, the amount granted to Vanuatu is rather small ($6.5 million or 4.9 million ECU), and it is not clear yet whether such modest funding can produce notable economic changes.

The STABEX program represents an interesting model for future commodity price stabilization schemes. Like some cartel arrangements (the ICAs, for example), STABEX has sought cooperation from both producing and consuming nations. But unlike most cartel initiatives, the EU's program has not tried to alter the path of commodity prices. Nonetheless, STABEX has been more effective than most cartels in achieving higher export revenues for the producers that it represents. The appeal of STABEX to European taxpayers, who are effectively footing the bill for the organization's subsidies, is uncertain. In essence, STABEX has addressed only one side of the problem of commodity market instability. Although developing nations receive subsidies to offset the effects of weak commodity prices, the program does nothing to address the economic dislocations that arise when commodity prices rise too quickly. In this regard, STABEX is inferior to a functioning buffer stock, by which both price increases and decreases are controlled.

Alternative Trade Organizations: Innovative Proposals for Changing the Terms of Commodity Trade

A number of firms and nongovernmental organizations (NGOs) have attempted to improve the terms of trade of developing nations. Typically, these alternative trade organizations (ATOs) seek to stabilize the trade revenues of exporting nations by purchasing their products at subsidized prices. The coverage tends to be quite broad, encompassing both commodities and labor-intensive handicrafts. While admirable, the effectiveness of these programs has been relatively small in relation to the overall volume of trade. This has much to do with the paucity of funding, which has been even more limited than that of governmental initiatives such as STABEX. In addition, the private foundations and institutions typically rely on consumers in the industrialized world to purchase the items at above-market prices.

Madeley (1992, 147–157) provided a detailed analysis of several corporate and nongovernmental ATOs. The organization Traidcraft, created in Great Britain in 1979, emphasizes a Christian view of international trade whose focus is justice, not profitability. Traidcraft has facilitated the import of coffee, tea, food products, textiles, and clothing from developing nations (a total of 5.5 million pounds in 1991), mainly to churches in England. A similar entity, also based in the United Kingdom, is Oxfam Trading, which markets many products from developing countries—including handicrafts and furnishings, as well as commodities such as coffee, cocoa, tea, honey, and nuts—directly to the public through hundreds of small storefronts. In 1991, its sales reached 16 million pounds. Oxfam Trading relies on consumers to pay somewhat higher prices in order to contribute to an improved standard of living in the producing countries.

A completely different approach is taken by the London-based Third World Information Network (TWIN), which provides consulting services and technical support to producers in developing nations. TWIN's major focus has been on improving the profitability of trade in coffee, particularly in reaction to the collapse of the International Coffee Organization in the late 1980s. The group has also cooperated with Traidcraft, Oxfam, and other NGOs to promote more favorable terms of trade for coffee exporters in light of the failures of the cartel system.

Similar foundations promoting the sale of products from the developing world have formed elsewhere in Europe, as well as in the United States and Canada (Madeley 1992, 186–188). Despite the conscientious efforts of groups such as the Indiana-based Friends of the Third World and the Equal Exchange in Massachusetts, the NGOs have affected little change on the total trade between the industrialized and developing nations.

In addition to the work of the alternative trade organizations, some corporations have worked to subsidize the trade of developing nations. The Body Shop, for example, sells products (ranging from the fairly exotic to the mundane) manufactured in Brazil, India, and Nepal. Although most of the items marketed through such corporate sponsorship have been handicrafts, some commodity products (or items derived from commodities) have also been subsidized.

COMMODITY PRICE INSTABILITY AND THE DIFFERENTIATION BETWEEN RENEWABLE AND NONRENEWABLE RESOURCES

If stability in international commodity markets is to be attained, it is imperative that the fundamental differences in products and producers be recognized. For goods, this differentiation must take into account the separate trade issues that exist for renewable and nonrenewable resources. For renewable commodities such as cocoa, coffee, and rubber, production remains concentrated in a few nations, and yet oversupply remains a perennial problem. Both consumers and producers must work together to tackle the problem of stabilizing the export earnings of developing countries that rely on a narrow range of agricultural and tropical products. As for nonrenewable resources such as bauxite, petroleum, and tin, it is likely that prices will rise significantly as shortages of these raw materials develop. Since the industrialized world has the most to lose when prices surge, it must work diligently to secure market stability and avoid another round of commodity inflation.

A distinction must also be drawn between commodities that are produced exclusively in the developing world versus those that are exported by both developing and developed nations. While price stabilization programs for goods produced in Africa, Latin America, and the Pacific Rim can be regarded as a just way of transferring wealth to impoverished nations, price controls for commodities emanating from both these regions and industrialized countries only reinforce the existing disparities in export earnings (this would have been the case had UNCTAD successfully implemented its plan to cartelize the copper, cotton, and sugar markets). Under the assumption that the financial resources available to address the problems faced by commodity producers will always be limited, it would be far better to target subsidies for products that are specific to the developing world (e.g., bauxite, cocoa, coffee, rubber, and tin).

COOPERATIVE ARRANGEMENTS WITHIN THE DEVELOPING WORLD

Securing Known Prices Within Existing Trading Systems

As argued in chapter 3, futures markets provide a reasonable alternative to cartel agreements, provided that the goal is to secure stable prices rather than to raise prices from trend. Verleger (1994, 140–144) argued that commodity producers should be making full use of both futures contracts and other financial instruments that provide price guarantees. The author noted, with dismay, that operatives within OPEC have been unwilling to utilize futures markets for fear that a miscalculation will be made and a career possibly ruined. The finance ministers of the OPEC nations have argued that their countries lack the resources to make the margin payments on their expected production, which for Saudi Arabia alone would have totaled nearly $3 billion in 1993. Verleger also advocated the use of options to guarantee prices, a tactic that Mexico used successfully in 1991 to secure its oil revenues.

Verleger suggested that petroleum producers consider pursuing other financial derivatives, such as swap agreements, as a means of stabilizing exports. This strategy calls for the exporting nation to promise compensation to the importing country if the price of petroleum should rise above a certain per-barrel price. Conversely, if the price were to fall below a certain strike price, the importer would compensate the exporter. The result would be a substantial reduction in risk for both trading partners.

Although Verleger made a strong case for the use of hedging to eliminate the uncertainties faced by exporting nations, this proposal does not address long-term deterioration of markets. In the case of erratically declining prices such as those faced by Ghana and other cocoa producers, for example, futures markets provide a means of disposing output at known prices, but the underlying problem of overproduction can simply reemerge in the next harvest. As will be discussed below, there are more permanent solutions to the problem of excess supply that can benefit both the producing and consuming nations.

Reducing Competition in International Commodity Markets Through Regional Planning

One of the most significant trends in international commerce of this century has been the formation of regional trading arrangements. Since the first free trade area (FTA) was created with the founding of the European Economic Community in 1957 (effected with the signing of the Treaty of Rome), many other common markets have emerged, most in the developing world (LeClair 1997). The Caribbean Community (CARICOM), the Latin American Integration Association (LAIA), the Association of Southeast Asian Nations (ASEAN), and the Southern Market (MERCOSUR) all have as their primary goal the promotion of increased regional trade between member states through the removal of tariffs and other barriers to trade. In many instances, however, the lowering of trade barriers has acted as a springboard to increased cooperation on development.

The nations of MERCOSUR—Argentina, Brazil, Paraguay, and Uruguay—while still focused primarily on trade issues, have committed themselves to an ambitious plan of joint economic development that includes significant regional planning. These objectives were articulated in a mission statement released from the Uruguayan Embassy: "Coordination of macroeconomic and sectorial policies of member states relating to foreign trade, agriculture, industry, taxes, monetary system, exchange and capital, services, customs, transport and communications..." ("Objectives of MERCOSUR"). By conferring with one another on which sectors of their economies are being developed, the members of this common market work to avoid the destructive intraregional competition that has plagued producers in the cocoa, coffee, rubber, and sugar markets in the past.

For the nations of LAIA—Argentina, Brazil, Chile, Ecuador, Mexico, Paraguay, Peru, and Uruguay—the advancement of intraregional trade has been expanded to include bilateral agreements between member states. For example, in the course of the decade following the formation of the FTA in 1980, Argentina and Brazil signed twenty-four protocols, the first of which called for a common market for capital goods, even to the extent of reciprocal investments by the two governments. The two countries also collaborated on research and development and food production. The trade initiatives of LAIA provide a model for cooperative rather than contentious development of critical export markets.

A similar set of objectives motivated Indonesia, Malaysia, the Philippines, Singapore, and Thailand to band together to form ASEAN in 1967 (Brunei joined later, in 1984). Beyond the expected goal of reducing or eliminating tariffs, the members of the FTA signed three major accords— the ASEAN Industrial Project, ASEAN Industrial Complementation, and the ASEAN Industrial Joint Venture—that encouraged a wide range of capital ventures. Had these proposals been realized, the manufacturing capabilities of the region would have been largely integrated. Like most common markets in the developing world, however, ASEAN's actual accomplishments fell far short of its stated goals. The possibility of meaningful alterations of production patterns for this FTA still exists. Particularly for the member states of Indonesia, Malaysia, and Thailand, whose economies have been seriously impacted by commodity price instability, ASEAN provides an arena within which long-range planning could help eliminate the deleterious effects of excess production.

Perhaps the most ambitious of the Latin American integration movements was CARICOM, an association of twelve Caribbean nations that formed in 1973 as a successor organization to the Caribbean Free Trade

Association. The charter of CARICOM demonstrates that beyond the creation of a free trade area, the signatories sought to reduce or eliminate regional market competition through a wide range of joint economic programs. The goal of localized development was most stridently expressed in Article III of CARICOM's protocol of June 1998, in which the members of the FTA pledged to pursue the following: the sharing of natural resources, personnel, technology, and management capabilities; linkages among economic sectors and enterprises within and among member states; regional economic projects capable of achieving scales of production; and the diversification of products and markets for goods and services with a view to increasing the range and value of exports. The protocol also defined the responsibilities of the newly formed Council for Trade and Economic Development, which was to "collaborate with competent agencies to assist Member States in designing appropriate policy instruments to support industries, which may include effective export promotion policies, financing policies, incentives and technological policies" (CARICOM Protocol of 1998). In addition, the council was charged with promoting coordinated research and development within CARICOM.

The stated goals of CARICOM can serve as a trade model for developing nations that are dependent on export revenues from commodities. Owing to the scarcity of mineral deposits or climatic growing conditions, the production of commodities such as bauxite, cocoa, coffee, natural rubber, and tin tends to be concentrated in equatorial regions. In the case of renewable agricultural and tropical commodities, there is no easy means of constraining production from one growing season to the next. The clustered exporters of these products should work together with their neighbors to coordinate current and future output levels and thereby avoid unmanageable surpluses and damaging competition. The same spirit of cooperation could be extended to the region's producers of nondurable manufactured goods (e.g., textiles and apparel). By fostering an atmosphere of cooperation on investment, planning, and production, commodity-exporting nations can collectively restructure trade and possibly solve the vexing problem of persistent market instability.

COMMODITY TRADE ASSOCIATIONS

The history of the cartel movement in the 1970s provides some valuable lessons on the difficulties of establishing cooperative trade agreements. In retrospect, it was inevitable that when the producers of coffee and tin followed the advice of UNCTAD and formed partnerships with consuming nations to stabilize their markets, the quest for higher prices would conflict with the desire for stable prices. It is widely recognized that, with the exception of petroleum, the developing nations suffer far more serious economic consequences from falling commodity prices than the industrialized nations experience from rising prices. The inherent imbalance in economic risks between producing and consuming countries might induce exporters to band together to address market instability without the participation of their trading partners.

In order to secure dependable prices, the exporting countries must eliminate surpluses and avoid the tendency to diversify trade by simply offering another overproduced commodity. Once again, a distinction must be made between renewable and nonrenewable resources. The producers of bauxite, petroleum, and tin, for example, can regulate their rate of extraction to match predetermined production levels. For exporters of goods such as cocoa and coffee, output is largely determined by climatic factors, and so establishing quotas is more difficult. To better serve their own interests, nations that produce agricultural products should not export beyond established levels.

In addition, diversification efforts within the developing world should be coordinated. Specifically, in markets that are especially susceptible to excess production, the exporters could consider joining forces to seize the lion's share of world output and exercise their market prerogatives. Working together, these trade cooperatives could discourage the entry of new producers into their markets by offering these potential competitors incentives toward the development of other products. These incitements could include the sharing of technological and human resources and the pledge to support the new products through purchase agreements.

Potential Producer Associations

The grouping of potential associations of producers of cocoa, coffee, rubber, and tin and their combined shares of total trade are presented in Table 5.6. Based on current production levels, these hypothetical associations would control most of world production if they decided to work as trading blocks. Although coffee production is the most dispersed of the products included, its nine producers would control 69.6 percent of the market (including most of the trade of the more valuable arabica beans). A seven-member cooperative cocoa agreement would incorpo-

Table 5.6

Potential Commodity Trade Arrangements (with potential percentages of world output)

Producer	Cocoa	Coffee	Rubber	Tin
Australia				4.4
Bolivia				7.7
Brazil		7.4	26.8	9.0
Cameroon	4.1			
China			6.0	27.8
Columbia		12.4		
Costa Rica		2.4		
Ethiopia			3.9	
Ghana		14.7		
Guatemala		3.6		
India			8.1	
Indonesia	10.5	7.4	23.8	20.5
Ivory Coast	39.5	4.0		
Malaysia	4.5		19.2	3.4
Mexico			5.4	
Nigeria		5.6		
Peru				11.9
Russia				5.3
Sri Lanka			1.8	
Thailand		3.7	30.1	
Uganda				
Totals	86.3	69.6	89.0	90.0

Note: Figures are drawn from those presented in chapter 2.

rate a sizable 86.3 percent of total production. The degree of concentration in the international tin market would be even greater, with eight nations controlling 90 percent of production. Just six nations producing natural rubber could control 89 percent of world output.

The possibility of cooperative organizations forming in other commodity markets seems less likely. In the case of both petroleum and sugar, production is both dispersed and not confined to the developing world, both necessary conditions if associations of this sort are to function. For petroleum, there is the added problem of the existence of OPEC, whose members command the majority of world production. Finally, the unique situation that prevails in the international bauxite market suggests that a trade association would be both infeasible and unnecessary. The extraction and marketing of the ore is still carried out primarily by multinationals from the industrialized nations who are unlikely to cooperate in the management of supply. The host countries are satisfied with the boost in export levies imposed by the International Bauxite Association and are therefore unlikely to pursue a different form of cooperative action.

How Producer Associations Would Function

Unlike cartel arrangements in which members decide on a market price and the quotas necessary to enforce that price, producer associations must anticipate demand well into the future and adjust output accordingly. The cocoa and coffee markets, for example, would be especially well served by cooperative associations, for they have been in the throes of sustained declines that have driven down prices, and the surpluses will only worsen if current production levels are maintained.[5] Exporters of natural rubber must recognize that their long-term prospects are compromised by price increases that only encourage the production of synthetics in the developed world. Finally, tin is a required element in only a few products such as soldering compounds and metal plating; price gouging will only lead to the substitution of cheaper materials (e.g., the use of plastic instead of tin for the coating of the interior of food cans and for the protective covers of wine bottles). The producers of tin must accept the inevitability of continued, diminished demand and curtail production or risk declining terms of trade.

Once a reasonable forecast of future demand has been made, output in these trade groups would be allocated according to the producer's existing share of the world market and to their degree of dependence on the export. This assessment would be best calculated according to distinctions between producers. The Ivory Coast and Guatemala, for example, control only a small fraction of total coffee production, yet they rely heavily on the resulting export earnings. Brazil, on the other hand, produces over one-fourth of the world's coffee but enjoys a highly diversified export base. Similar divergences of export shares exist in the cocoa, coffee, rubber, and tin markets.

Any cooperative market ventures would also have to address the effects of business cycles on the demand for commodities, especially industrial inputs such as rubber and tin. For example, when Western Europe, Japan, and the United States slipped into a recession between 1991 and 1992, automobile sales plunged and the demand for natural rubber plummeted. If the producing countries had worked together to cut output during this downturn, the price of rubber would not have fallen so dramatically.

In addition to coordinating short- and long-term supply, a producer cooperative could, in some cases, foster the vertical integration of commodity-exporting nations. The potential value of a given commodity is generally not fully realized if the good is exported in an unprocessed, unpackaged form. Much of the value-added of the petroleum industry, for example, is created when oil is processed beyond its initial state, as in gasoline or kerosene. The same pricing structure of raw versus processed materials holds true for bauxite and, to a lesser degree, tin and rubber. As demonstrated in chapter 3, raw material exporters have seen the terms of trade move against them for two decades at the same time that producers of processed commodities have enjoyed stable relative prices.

Unlike cartels or even futures markets, producer cooperatives offer a promising solution to the persistent problems of permanent oversupply and declining prices in commodity markets, particularly those of cocoa, coffee, and sugar. The next section will present an even more radical means of leveling the playing field in international trade.

COMMODITY CLEARINGHOUSES

A more drastic, and fundamentally anticompetitive, approach to the goal of securing higher prices and constraining supply would be the development of clearinghouses for each of the primary commodity markets. To date, the use of "central points of sale" has been confined to transcontinental corporations as an instrument of monopolization. It is through strictly controlled points of distribution that the international supplies and prices of diamonds and uranium ore (deposits of which are fairly widely dispersed) have been monitored. What follows is a discussion of the formation and relative effectiveness of these arrangements (the similar controls put in place in the gold and silver ore markets are beyond the scope of this study).

The DeBeers Corporation

The DeBeers Corporation has its founding in the ambition and, many would say, avariciousness, of Cecil Rhodes, an Englishman who in the 1870s saw in the abundant diamond holdings of the Vaal River region of South Africa the possibility of untold wealth (for a recent treatment of the DeBeers cartel, see Spar 1994, 39–87). In 1880, Rhodes bought partial control of the DeBeers diamond mine, one of the most productive of the many South African deposits of the gemstone. As early as the 1870s, the rich yields of these diamond fields had begun to depress international prices. Rhodes realized that in order to protect his new enterprise and also safeguard the long-term profitability of the diamond industry, it was imperative that he work to preserve and expand the mass perception that diamonds were scarce and, therefore, inherently valuable.

To achieve his objective, Rhodes needed to control both the production and distribution of diamonds, and he soon concluded that the only means of securing absolute price stability was to attempt to establish a single source for diamonds. Thus, in 1887 Rhodes bought out the mine's other claim holders to secure complete control of the DeBeers operation, and a year later, in 1888, he purchased the Kimberley Mine, the other major source of South African diamonds. With the only other sizable known reserves at the time located in Brazil, his acquisition of most of the world's diamond production was completed.

As for distribution, Rhodes worked through a coalition of South African merchants known as the Diamond Syndicate, whose members saw the advantages to be gained by joining in on the monopoly and purchasing diamonds in quantities and prices set by him. With this controlled point of apportionment or clearinghouse in place, Rhodes had a permanent means of manipulating demand and coordinating supply.

The modern DeBeers cartel has deviated very little from the principles of tight market restriction and fabricated scarcity established by its founder. Through its London-based Central Selling Organization, the DeBeers Corporation maintains its control of the sale of 80 to 85 percent of the world's uncut diamonds (this despite the fact that the company's South African mines produce only 8 percent of world output). Through a vast network of interlocking corporations and punitive contracts overseen by the DeBeers Corporation, the world's producers collectively maintain stockpiles, adjust output, and ensure the sale of all types and qualities of stones produced, all in an effort to ensure that diamond prices bear no relation to the cost of production. One cannot discount the publicity end of the cartel; the familiar and effective advertisements that bombard U.S. consumers are a testament to the enduring belief that a one-carat diamond is the ultimate expression of love.

In a lesson never learned by the coffee-exporting nations, the DeBeers organization (beginning with Rhodes) realized that controlling the price of top-notch stones also required the control of prices for lower-grade diamonds. Diamonds of inferior quality are substitutes for larger and flawless stones, and so depressed prices at the low end of the market will result in downward pressure on prices at the high end. To avoid this tendency toward substitution, the cartel mixes the lots of diamonds distributed through its London clearinghouse, thereby forcing its merchants to sell the full range of stones produced. In contrast, the International Coffee Agreements of the 1970s and 1980s established export controls on arabica beans, but left the market for lower-grade robusto beans to its own devices. As the ICAs pushed the price of coffee beans upward, the robusto beans became more attractive to buyers and the cartel's ability to manage prices beyond the short term was permanently effected.

By the mid-1950s, diamond production in South Africa had begun to wane, and the output from mines beyond the control of DeBeers—those in other African countries, Australia, and the former Soviet Union—was seriously damaging the cartel's ability to control the industry. In order to rein in its competition, DeBeers has, over the years, formed alliances and negotiated treaties (ranging from heavy-handed to conciliatory) with governments and firms that produce diamonds. A distributor that violates the cartel's pricing arrangements might well find that its next lot of diamonds is packed with stones of inferior quality. Producers that have tried to defect from the Central Selling Organization are subjected to the cartel's wrath. (As related by Spar 1994, 62–63, in the case of Zaire's renouncement of the cartel in 1981, the market was inexplicably flooded with the contents of a stockpile that drove the market price of industrial diamonds—the type of diamond produced by the African nation—down by nearly 50 percent.) It is the punitive aspect of the diamond consortium that makes its trade policies fundamentally different from the collusive arrangements that have formed around other commodities. The centralized, authoritarian hierarchy of clearinghouses of the sort used by the DeBeers Corporation runs counter to the principles of free trade. Nonetheless, for commodities with high concentration ratios (e.g., cocoa), the model set by the diamond consortium may provide an attractive alternative to traditional cartels.

The International Uranium Cartel

Even more than that of the DeBeers Corporation, the history of the uranium cartel is shrouded in secrecy (Spar 1994, 88–136). In fact, even the cartel's founders remain unknown, although some believe that it was the British multinational firm of Rio Tinto Zinc, working through subsidiaries and joint participation on corporate boards, that oversaw the vastly dispersed mining interests of uranium ore.

The exploitable deposits of uranium are concentrated in Australia, Canada, South Africa, Sweden, and the United States. France also plays a pivotal role, for it controls the output of uranium from three secondary producers in Africa, all of them former colonies. In the 1960s, the uranium industry experienced a significant problem with overproduction and weakening prices. By 1971, the price of uranium ore had fallen to a low of $3.55 per pound, but prices then rebounded, reaching a high of $55 per pound in 1980 (Spar 1994, 91). Although the inflation of uranium prices can be attributed, in part, to increased demand of the ore as an input in the nuclear power industry, it has more to do with the effects of cartelization.

Under the guise of an informational session, a consortium of uranium producers, including representatives from Australia, Canada, France, and South Africa, along with industry leaders from twenty-four mining companies, met in Paris in 1972 and agreed to establish a minimum price for the ore. With this accord, Australia, Canada, and France were skirting along the boundaries of trade legality. For its part, the Canadian government established mandated quotas and floor prices that just happened to conform to those set by the cartel. By placing the export sale of uranium under government regulation, the Cabinet protected Canadian companies from prosecution under the nation's antitrust legislation. Initially, the price increase sought by the cartel was modest (less than $2 per pound), yet plans for more significant price increases were soon in place. All purchase requests for uranium were directed to the office of the Commissioner of Atomic Energy in Paris, where demand was divvied up among consortium members. Ostensibly, a bidding process was followed, but the victor was actually predetermined by officials at this central selling point. In this respect, the uranium cartel was not unlike the collusive agreement established in the U.S. electrical equipment industry in the 1950s in which prices were raised by subverting what appeared to be a competitive bidding process (a fundamental difference being that officers of the American transformer firms were eventually prosecuted for antitrust violations).

As early as 1972, details of the uranium cartel's activities were becoming widely known. Between 1976 and 1977, the Westinghouse Corporation, a maker of light-water nuclear reactors that require uranium as an input, successfully sued the members of the cartel over the rise in the commodity's price (the settlement was made out of court). While this legal action certainly contributed to the dissolution of the cartel, conditions within the uranium market had also fundamentally changed by the late 1970s, when prices firmed in response to increased demand. Worried about further prosecutive action and comfortable with market prices, uranium-producing firms decided not to risk any further involvement in the collusive agreement.

The pricing mechanism of the uranium cartel was quite similar to that of the diamond cartel. Prices were predetermined at a clearinghouse, and the buyer could either accept the stated price or suffer the consequences of circumventing the cartel (the retributions mainly taking the form of reduced availability of adequate supplies).

A common feature of both the diamond and uranium consortiums was the use of a clearinghouse to strictly regulate sales on the international market. In contrast, none of the international commodity agreements discussed in chapter 3 utilized an arrangement of this type. It is not surprising that a system that utilizes a single selling point and coercion can exert a greater degree of control than a program that imposes only loosely enforced export and production agreements.

Clearinghouses and the Concentration of Trade

From the viewpoint of commodity producers in the developing world, clearinghouses might have served as viable alternatives to cartels in the turbulent markets of the 1970s and early 1980s. In the cocoa market, for example, the ineffectualness of cartelization was illustrated by the International Cocoa Agreements of the 1970s, which were rendered nonbinding because of tightening supplies and prices that rose above target levels. The binding ICCA of 1981 set new target prices and limited exports, but even with the significant augmentation of its buffer stocks, the cartel failed to firm prices and the collusive agreement soon fell apart. Had the producers of the highly concentrated cocoa market banded together and channeled their output through a clearinghouse, the importing nations would have been forced to pay the target price. In order to maintain the floor prices, the central selling point for cocoa would have had to store surpluses in the 1980s, when demand fell and production soared, but this expense would have been comparable to the costs of the buffer stock purchases made by the cartel during this period. Market equilibrium would have been restored in the 1990s, when output more closely matched the international demand for cocoa.

A centralized marketing mechanism would have been even more ben-eficial to the members of the International Coffee Organization, whose output was especially plagued by the problems of variation in product quality. As noted earlier, by failing to regulate the market for robusto beans, the ICAs of the 1970s and 1980s unwittingly permitted down-ward pressure on the price of the more profitable arabica coffees. A clearinghouse would have marketed both grades of coffee and therefore the decline in robusto prices would have been prevented. Although the concentration ratio in the coffee market in the 1970s was lower than that of the cocoa market, the top eight producers of the former commodity could have effectively seized control of world production had they cre-ated a central point of sale.

The pursuit of centralized marketing strategies would have been even more advantageous for the bauxite, petroleum, and tin producers. Free of the need to store surplus production in times of lowered demand, a clearinghouse for tin, for example, could have established both a target price and the production levels necessary to attain that price. World out-put could have been split among the producers (in much the same way that the uranium cartel divided its market).

The establishment of central selling points is desirable only for ex-porting nations. For the industrialized countries that rely on commodity imports, distribution centers of this kind pose the threat of increased prices and inflexible market conditions.

CONCLUSION

Although the markets for commodities have been remarkably quiescent since the mid-1980s, renewed turmoil is a strong possibility as agricul-tural supplies are tightened and reserves of raw materials are strained. In markets for renewable products like cocoa, coffee, sugar, and rubber, demand may overwhelm the productive capacity of exporting nations. In the case of nonrenewable resources such as bauxite, petroleum, and tin, the dwindling output of known deposits could create serious long-term shortages. Should production falter and prices rise precipitously, the general level of prosperity enjoyed in the world at the threshold of the new millennium could be jeopardized.

This chapter has focused on the array of programs that have sought to improve the terms of trade that face developing nations. The most note-worthy of the governmental systems, STABEX, has transferred monetary resources to exporting countries but has not been able to solve the problem of perennial overproduction. Private efforts to improve economic conditions in the developing world include the ATOs, whose grassroots, humanitarian efforts have focused on changing the fortunes of small-scale producers one at a time.

Perhaps the most promising means of achieving a permanent and wide-scale solution to the problem of overproduction lie in the concepts of regional cooperation and producer cooperatives, both of which strive to coordinate long-term planning among commodity exporters. A proven, but ultimately destructive, means of market manipulation is the use of clearinghouses. But despite the attractiveness that this market device might hold for commodity exporters, especially those with high concentration ratios, the use of a central selling point would elevate trade revenues in the short run at the risk of raising the ire of the industrialized nations. In the long run, the widespread use of clearinghouses could lead to trade conflicts and the accelerated substitution of alternative materials for commodities.

The most probable path for resource markets in the next fifty years leads toward continued reliance on free trade coupled with the use of futures markets to protect both exporters and importers. Current trends suggest that the terms of trade will continue to move against exporting nations in the medium term, a situation that could be avoided through even a modest degree of cooperation between producers. If the industrialized countries fail to support the diversification of commodity output in the developing world, significant economic disruptions will almost certainly become a feature of trade in the twenty-first century.

NOTES

1. The figure for Thailand is misleading, as this nation has ceased to aggressively mine and market tin, presumably as a consequence of the weakness in prices since 1985. A rebound in prices would undoubtedly induce Thailand to raise production levels.

2. Technically, in estimating the effect that rising production has on demand, one should control for the price of the commodity, yet empirical tests suggest that (with the exception of the petroleum market) the link between prices and demand is weak.

3. The larger coefficient for rubber is a reflection of the dramatic changes in demand for automobiles as a result of rising GDP. In addition, it should be noted that, unlike the other estimations presented, the price of rubber did not significantly affect demand.

4. Much of the following information was taken from "The STABEX System and Export Revenues in ACP Countries," European Commission, 1997.

5. This may not necessarily be true for cocoa in the longer term. In 1999, a fungus began to take hold in the cocoa groves, threatening future supplies. The resulting higher prices will, of course, be of little comfort to those nations that have lost trees.

REFERENCES

Hewitt, A. 1983. "STABEX: An Evaluation of the Economic Impact over the First Five Years." *World Development* 2: 1005–1027.
LeClair, M. 1997. *Regional Integration and Global Free Trade*. Brookfield, VT: Avebury Press.
Madeley, J. 1992. *Trade and the Poor*. New York: St. Martin's Press.
Spar, D. 1994. *The Cooperative Edge*. Ithaca: Cornell University Press.
Verleger, P. 1994. *Adjusting to Volatile Energy Prices*. Washington, DC: Institute for International Economics.

Index

About the Author

Mark S. LeClair is an Associate Professor of Economics at Fairfield University in Fairfield, Connecticut, where he teaches international trade and finance and mathematical economics. Professor LeClair is the author of *Regional Integration and Global Free Trade: Addressing the Fundamental Conflicts* (1997). He has also published works in the areas of corporate support for the arts and culture and on the validity of methods that are used to value closely held firms.